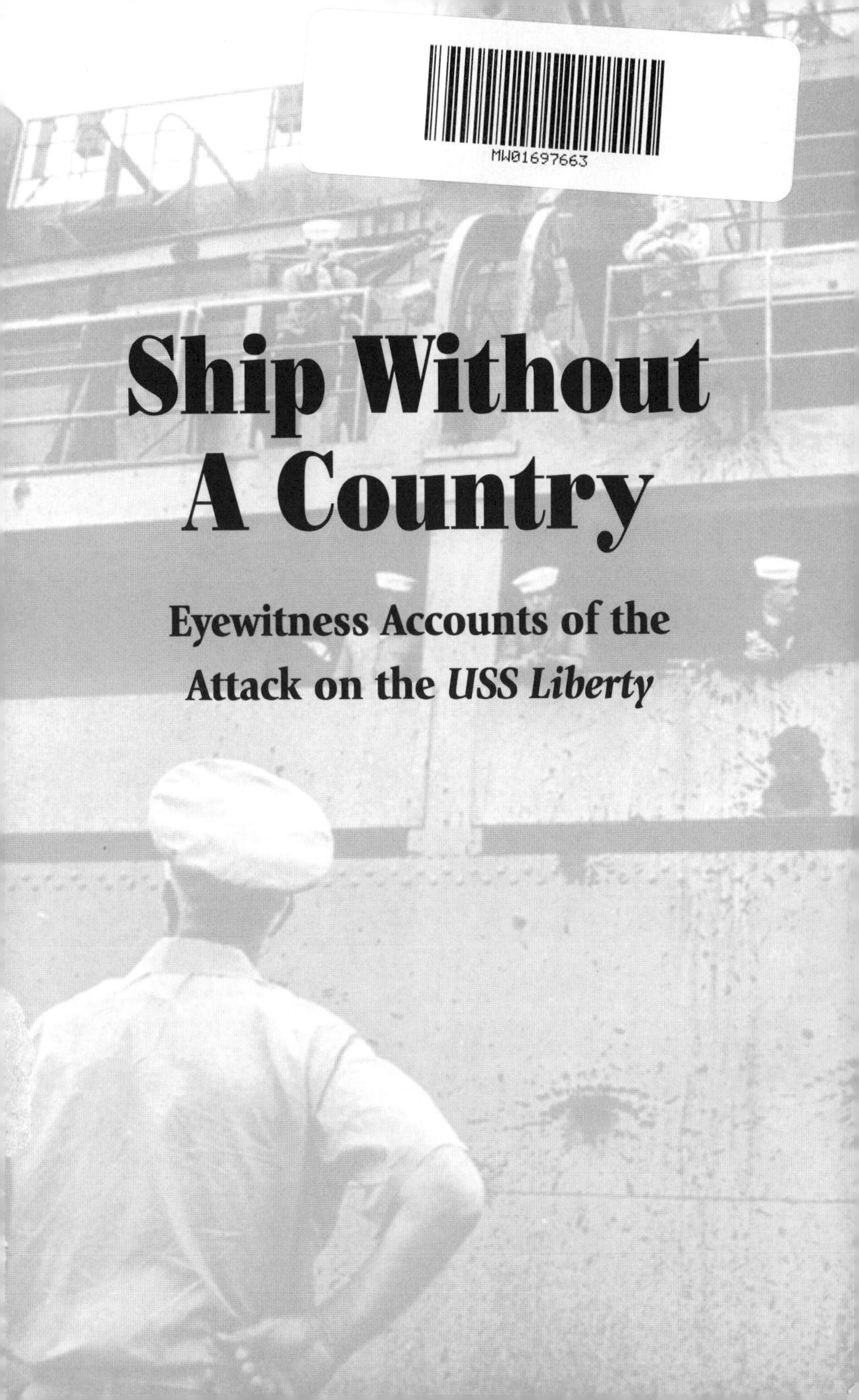

Ship Without A Country

Eyewitness Accounts of the Attack on the *USS Liberty*

Ship Without a Country

Eyewitness Accounts of the Attack on the *USS Liberty*

ISBN 978-0-9818086-6-6

Published by

AMERICAN FREE PRESS

645 Pennsylvania Avenue SE
Suite 100
Washington, D.C. 20003
www.americanfreepress.net
1-888-699-NEWS toll free

In conjunction with **SISYPHUS PRESS**
P.O. Box 10495
State College, PA
16805-0495

And **CRESCENT & CROSS**
JTB Publications
Box 27
Careywood, ID
83809 USA

First Edition: September 2009: 3,000 copies

Special Consultant: Phil Tourney
Cover design: Peter Currenti.
Manufactured in the United States of America

Ship Without A Country

Eyewitness Accounts of the Attack on the *USS Liberty*

By Victor Thorn & Mark Glenn

Published in 2009 by
American Free Press, Washington, D.C.

DEDICATION:

This book is dedicated to all those who lost their lives in—and to those who survived—the attack on the *USS Liberty* on June 8, 1967, and to those who have relentlessly pursued the truth about what really happened that fateful day. Both the living and the dead deserve the truth, not a never-ending whitewash.

—Victor Thorn & Mark Glenn

ABOUT THE AUTHORS:

Victor Thorn founded Sisyphus Press in the fall of 2000, and is the author of 12 major books, as well as 10 chapbooks. He has published the works of numerous writers in the alternative media, and has also produced four CD-ROMs and DVDs, including *Evidence of Revision*. Thorn is also the editor of four anthologies, and his political articles have appeared in various newspapers and magazines around the country. He was also co-host of *The Victor Thorn Show* on the Reality Radio Network from 2002-2003. In February 2004 he co-founded WING TV (World Independent News Group), which was a daily Internet television and radio talk show which was viewed in over 100 countries worldwide. Thorn has made hundreds of different radio and television appearances (including *Coast-to-Coast AM*, *The Lionel Show* on WOR 710), and has done a weekly one-hour news update on Alex Merklinger's *Mysteries of the Mind*, while also appearing weekly on Vyzygoth's *From the Grassy Knoll* radio show and Frank Whalen's *Frankly Speaking Radio*. Thorn has been an avid political activist who spoke at the OKC Bombing 10th anniversary, as well as protesting 9-11 in New York City and in front of the White House.

Mark Glenn, a former schoolteacher covering history and several foreign languages, joined the fray after years of reading *The Spotlight* and then *American Free Press*. Asked by AFP to join on as a regular correspondent in 2007, for several years he wrote weekly columns for the paper until 2009. He is the author of several books dealing with the threat posed by Zionism including *No Beauty in the Beast: Israel Without Her Mascara*. For several years he has been a regular on the Republic Broadcasting Network where, along with co-host and survivor of the *USS Liberty* Phil Tourney, he hosts *The Liberty Hour*, a 2-hour weekly radio program dealing with not only the attack on the *Liberty*, but how it all pertains to current events. Currently he resides in northern Idaho along with his wife Vicki and their nine children. His hard-hitting writings can be found at http://theuglytruth.wordpress.com. *No Beauty in the Beast* can be ordered from TBR, P.O. Box 15877, Washington, D.C. 20003 for $25 ppd.

Table of Contents

The Face of the Devil

BY MICHAEL COLLINS PIPER

Since 1948 there have been many crimes and conspiracies attributed or otherwise "connected" in some fashion to the state of Israel, ranging from the tragic terrorist attacks of September 11, 2001 to the assassination of President John F. Kennedy and on, even, to the bombing of the Murrah Building in Oklahoma City on April 19, 1995.

In truth, the list of allegations in this regard goes on and on. Israel,

---

LEFT: Two days after being attacked by Israeli military forces, the *USS Liberty* miraculously limped into port at Valletta, Malta. Captain William McGonagle inspects some of the extensive damage done to his ship, including massive torpedo strikes, rocket fire, and other holes in the hull and main deck. Bombed repeatedly, then napalmed, the captain refused to abandon his position on the bridge despite being seriously wounded. Surrounded by dozens of fellow crew members that had lost their lives, along with hundreds of other casualties, McGonagle and his men were still able to extinguish fires, battle floods, and overcome thick clouds of smoke that choked their ship. Enduring a nearly two-hour attack by the Israel Defense Forces (IDF), McGonagle manned his post for another 15 hours to ensure that the *Liberty* didn't sink after the unspeakable horrors it withstood. This photograph of McGonagle and his colleagues is a testament and record to the heroic survivors who, although battle-scarred and beaten, will never allow the world to forget what their murderous attackers had done to them.

its military and its intelligence services have proven grist for much speculation, some of it certainly well founded, some of it downright ridiculous.

But there is one thing which is absolutely indisputable: on June 8, 1967 the military forces of the state of Israel launched a deliberate and unprovoked attack on a virtually unarmed American intelligence ship, the *USS Liberty*, as it sailed peacefully on a sunny day in the Mediterranean, off the coast of Sinai, as the Stars and Stripes flapped fully visible in the breeze.

Then, as now, supporters of Israel in the United States and around the world, and certainly Israel itself, would say that using the word "deliberate" to describe the attack on an ally is not just an error, but an outrage. They will acknowledge the attack was deliberate, but hasten to add that Israel believed it was an Egyptian freighter that, so they say, bore a striking resemblance to the *Liberty*.

And there we come to the point of departure between those who believe the Israelis attacked the *Liberty* knowing full well it was an American vessel, and those who say otherwise.

Although in recent years Americans have been told to "support our troops" in various military ventures in the Middle East, there is precisely one group of troops whom it is not politically correct to support, and that is those troops—those survivors of the USS *Liberty*—who say that Israel's attack on the *Liberty* was indeed not only "deliberate," but that Israel knew the vessel belonged to the Jewish state's closest ally and patron, the United States.

There were 34 Americans killed that day by Israel, and more than 170 wounded. Some of the initial survivors later died due to complications arising from their injuries. Many spent difficult lives in the years that followed, suffering from not only the trauma of the event, but also as a direct consequence of what they (correctly) believed was their abandonment by a government of the United States eager to brush this matter under the rug.

Their views were supported by the fact that many people in high places, ranging from then-CIA Director Richard Helms, Secretary of State Dean Rusk, presidential advisor Clark Clifford (himself a longtime advocate for Israel in official Washington), and even to President Lyndon Johnson himself—among many, many others—who agreed absolutely with the *Liberty*'s survivors that the attack was carried out by Israel with full knowledge that it was an American ship they were so brutally firing upon, unleashing a hurricane of machine gun fire, napalm and torpedoes.

And it should be added that, as the evidence suggests—ranging from a broad variety of sources—the intent of Israel (along with a certain number of apparent collaborators inside the American government itself) was to sink the ship, kill all aboard, and then blame the massacre on Egypt, laying the pretext for an American military retaliation on that Arab country with which Israel was then at war.

The survivors, as we shall see, were told to "shut up" and not talk about what had happened. They were separated and scattered to other ships. And for many years those brave men—many of them bearing grievous wounds—did remain silent. But then, like ice beginning to thaw, they began to talk, slowly, and that's when the cover-up of the *Liberty* started to break.

While the attack on the *Liberty* did receive some coverage in the mass media in the days and weeks following the tragedy, the truth is that the media largely adopted a stance in agreement with the "official" version of events, suggesting that the attack was just a "tragic mistake" taking place during a time of war.

It wasn't until 1975 that a newly inaugurated weekly newspaper known as *The Spotlight* began publishing (over many years time) regular coverage of new developments surrounding increasing questions being raised by the survivors (and others) about the events of June 8,

1967 and the very real cover-up that followed. In fact, there were many prominent individuals who came forth, joining the chorus, asking for the truth to be told.

Although *The Spotlight* closed its doors in 2001, the former editors of that newspaper (myself among them) set up a new independent weekly, *American Free Press*, and that publication has picked up the torch and continued to demand justice for the men of the *Liberty* and for a full accounting—**a full, public accounting,** both by Israel and the United States.

Now, in this volume, two talented contributing editors to *American Free Press*—Victor Thorn and Mark Glenn—have joined forces with a host of *Liberty* survivors and others (high-ranking ex-diplomats and intelligence and military officers among them) to provide a remarkable overview of the story of the *Liberty* and the outrageous conduct of the U.S. and Israeli governments that followed.

It's not at any time a "nice" story, but a story which is nonetheless inspiring, for in these pages you will meet some very heroic people, both at the time and in years afterward, who have dared to speak out and confront very powerful forces determined to keep the facts about the *Liberty* from ever reaching a wide national audience, as it should.

When the story of the *Liberty* does come before enough people, it could prove to be the linchpin upon which very real reform of misguided U.S. policies in the Middle East—the ill-founded "special relationship" with the state of Israel—will finally come about.

The men of the *Liberty* saw the face of the devil that day, but they remain insistent that the truth must be told. It's our job to make sure the truth is known. This volume is one component in making that possible.

—MICHAEL COLLINS PIPER
Washington, D.C. 2009
September 16, 2009

War Crimes & Treason:

Israel's Deliberate Attack On the *USS Liberty*

BY VICTOR THORN

PART ONE—THE *USS LIBERTY*

June 8, 1967 was a clear, sunny day with unlimited visibility. It was such a nice day that as the *USS Liberty* floated in international waters 12½ miles north of the Sinai Peninsula, sailors sunbathed on the intelligence ship's deck. But all wasn't as tranquil as the sunlight would convey, for June 8 also marked the fourth day of the Six Day War that involved Israel, Egypt, Syria and Jordan.

Monitoring this situation was the *USS Liberty*, a World War II freighter converted into a spy vessel by the most secretive of all U.S. intelligence services, the National Security Agency (NSA). In fact, the *Liberty* was the most sophisticated and identifiable intelligence ship in the world at that time with dozens of large antennae, state of the art electronic intercept equipment, moon bounce satellite dishes, massive aerials, plus a TRSSCOM system that sent real-time messages to the National Security Agency. The *Liberty* also flew a large 5 x 8 foot American flag (40 square feet in size), was freshly painted with large white numbers and letters on its bow and hull, and contained only defensive weaponry, namely four 50-caliber machine guns suitable only for repulsing would-be boarders and pirates.

These details are important to keep in mind because, beginning at dawn, as the *Liberty* floated in international waters at less than five knots, a six-hour surveillance mission by low-flying, lumbering Israeli aircraft began. These reconnaissance planes flew at such low levels—sometimes as close as 200 feet—that they would rattle the deck of the ship. Sailors aboard the *Liberty*, seeing the Star of David prominently displayed on these surveillance aircraft and believing Israel was America's friend, waved to the Israeli pilots, as allies would normally do. Those commanding the Israeli surveillance planes not only identified this ship as being of American origin, they also positively identified it as being the *USS Liberty*.

PART TWO—THE ATTACK

Despite being fully aware of the *Liberty*'s status, at 2:00 in the afternoon the Jewish state unleashed the first wave of several murderous air assaults with three unmarked Mystere and Mirage III fighter jets pummeling the *Liberty* with rockets and cannon fire. First hit were the ship's antennae, electronics dishes, the four 50-caliber gun tubs and the American flag that was cut into ribbons of red, white and blue. As American sailors fled for cover, some of the *Liberty* crewmen hoisted another 5-by-8-foot flag to replace the previous one. It also was cut to pieces and later replaced with yet another flag, a seven-by-13-foot ceremonial one.

In the end, however, none of the flags proved effective in stopping the murderous assault as the Israelis sprayed the *Liberty* with napalm—a highly incendiary substance that sticks to everything it touches, including the flesh of those on the top deck of the ship that day.

While this unprovoked act of war was taking place, radio operators aboard the *Liberty* tried signaling for help. Their SOS distress messages were not heard, however, due to the fact Israel had deliberately jammed all five of the *Liberty*'s emergency radio channels—reserved solely for American use—a phenomenon proving beyond doubt the Jewish state was aware of who their target was beforehand and had previously zeroed in on it. To jam a stranger's radio in such a rapid manner without planning is virtually impossible.

Unable to get help, the *USS Liberty*, with six sailors already dead and 100+ wounded—including the ship's captain, William McGonagle—was a sitting duck for the military might of the Jewish state. Next, they sent in three boats loaded with the most deadly arsenal known to ships—torpedoes. With their target already in flames, the Israelis launched five of them, and although four missed their target, one hit the side of the ship, with devastating results. Twenty-five men were instantly killed.

As firefighters tried putting out fires from the napalm and damage control personnel attempted to save the wounded as they lay in pools of their own blood, they were under constant machine-gun fire from the torpedo boats, some of them only 50 feet away. After it was apparent the Israelis were intent on sinking the ship, Captain McGonagle gave a command: prepare to abandon ship. But as the surviving crewmen fled, Israeli torpedo boats, at close range, sprayed their life rafts with gunfire. It was a sickening display of brutality and savage inhumanity—a total lack of regard for human life. The Israeli's wanted no survivors.

Of the many miracles taking place that day was the fact that the *Liberty* did manage to get a short distress signal out. During the initial air attack, Israeli fighter pilots homed in on the operating antennae, while leaving others unscathed, including one that was later rigged with a coaxial cable to broadcast a call for help. Using their call sign—"Rockstar"—the *Liberty* declared it was under attack from unknown aircraft and requested assistance, a call that was picked up by the nearby Sixth Fleet. Fighter jets were immediately launched to rescue the ship.

But once the Sixth Fleet's commanding officer notified Washington, D.C. that rescue aircraft had been launched, Secretary of Defense Robert McNamara ordered the planes to be recalled. In fact, it was later reported that Robert McNamara was so irate when discovering that *Liberty* radiomen contacted the *USS America* that he barked, "Tell the Sixth Fleet to get those aircraft back immediately."

Fighter jets were launched again, only to be called back yet again from Washington, D.C. Had they arrived, the Israeli torpedo boats would have been obliterated and the 25 Americans blown to bits in the communications spaces would have been saved. As a result of this traitorous behavior, not only were 25 men needlessly killed; the remaining wounded had to wait a full 18 hours before help would arrive. It is the only instance in American naval history that a rescue mission was aborted while an American ship was under attack.

In all, the Israeli attack on America's *USS Liberty*—a ship that sat almost motionless in the water with no offensive weaponry while sailors sunbathed on its deck—lasted for almost two full hours, equal in length to the attack on Pearl Harbor, December 7, 1941. Close to 1,000 holes were found in the ship resulting from aircraft rockets and cannon fire—and a torpedo hole equal in size to an average American house.

Far more tragic, though, is the human loss that cannot be replaced in the same way as rocket and cannon holes can be patched and painted. 34 of America's finest were butchered that day, and 174 were wounded in what was the worst loss of naval personnel since World War II. Even though U.S. Secretary of State Dean Rusk, and later Joint Chiefs of Staff

Admiral Thomas Moorer, called this attack deliberate, to this day not one guilty party in Israel or the U.S. has been brought to justice.

PART THREE—ISRAELI LIES

Before proceeding, one thing should be made perfectly clear. What occurred on June 8th, 1967 was an unmitigated act of war perpetrated against the people of the United States by the state of Israel. It wasn't just a war crime against one ship carrying 294 American men, but an act of war against EVERY SINGLE AMERICAN ALIVE AT THAT TIME. Adding insult to injury, not only does Israel continue their made-to-order lies to this day; they have the audacity to place the blame on America. A case in point is Brigadier General Yiftah Spector, who flew a Mirage III fighter jet code named "Kursa" and who was the first pilot to reach the *USS Liberty*. In his exact words, "As far as I know, the mistake was of the *USS Liberty* for being there in the first place."

But this is only the first of many cowardly lies told by the Jewish state in covering up their treachery. Now, many years later, it has been proven beyond question that American radio operators in Spain, Lebanon, Crete, Germany and Vietnam heard the Israeli pilots in real time report that they recognized the ship they were ordered to attack as American; a revelation confirmed by U.S. Ambassador Dwight Porter, who had access to radio monitors at the U.S. Embassy in Lebanon.

If all this proves impossible to swallow, consider what Major Seth Mintz—in the Tel Aviv war room during the attacks—had to say: "Every person in that room knew without a doubt it was an American ship, and that it was the *USS Liberty*. There were many comments about the markings, about the extra large U.S. flag. There was never any discussion about the ship not being American. But General

Moshe Dayan ordered the attack anyway. We Israelis were guilty of an outrage." Senior Israeli pilot Evan Toni testified to former Congressman Pete McCloskey that while on air patrol that day, he immediately recognized the *USS Liberty*, informed headquarters of its status, and was told to *ignore the American flag and attack*. When he refused and returned to base, he was arrested on the spot for refusing to follow orders. Another pilot confirmed this report, stating that orders came directly from the IDF—Israeli Defense Forces—to attack the *Liberty*, and when he said that he saw an American flag, the response from headquarters was clear: "ATTACK IT."

Israel's swarm of lies continued afterward. The first was that there had been only one aircraft involved in the attack, and that the *Liberty* was sailing at high speed. It should be noted that the *Liberty* was floating at only five knots, and when it limped into dry dock in Malta almost six days later, it was filled with thousands of rocket and cannon fire holes, to say nothing of the cavern in its side caused by the torpedo blast, not something a single aircraft could have achieved as Israel claimed.

An even more outrageous lie was Israel's claim that they mistook the *Liberty* for an Egyptian ship, the *El Quseir*, used to ferry horses decades earlier. Even a superficial examination of this fairy tale reveals it to be an obvious fabrication. First, there were no Egyptian naval exercises that day. Secondly, the *Liberty* was almost four times the size of the *El Quseir*, and with its 45 antennae, was totally different in appearance. Third, Egyptian ships have their numbers painted in black and in Arabic, while U.S. ships paint their letters in white and in the English language (using the Roman alphabet). Finally, the same American life rafts shot at close range by Israeli torpedo boats clearly had "U.S. Navy" written on them. Any member of the Israeli Defense Forces would be familiar with such distinctions.

But the evidence doesn't end there. Unbeknownst to Israel at the time, on June 8th, 1967 the U.S. Navy had a top-secret EC-121 Warning Star intelligence aircraft flying overhead the *USS Liberty* that recorded the entire affair. When the IDF discovered the whereabouts of this surveillance plane, they gave orders to shoot it from the sky. In yet another example of the many miracles taking place that day, the EC-121 evaded Israeli missiles.

With all of this information in mind, the most obvious question is: who ordered these attacks on the *Liberty*? The answer, quite simply, is Israeli Defense Minister General Moshe Dayan, who served under Prime Minister Levi Eshkol. This explosive news has been confirmed by many different sources, including a CIA report categorically stating: "Dayan personally ordered the attack on the ship, and one of his generals adamantly opposed the action, saying, 'This is pure murder'."

But Moshe Dayan, in addition to being a cold-blooded murderer, was also a liar, as evidenced by his assertion that he commanded the Israeli air force to cease and desist their attack as soon as they saw U.S. lettering on the *Liberty*. The fact of the matter is quite different, however, as they kept firing well beyond that point, and only quit when they ran out of ammo. Moshe Dayan is a truly despicable human being, and should go down in the annals of history as a war criminal on a par with any Communist butcher.

PART FOUR—U.S. GOVERNMENT COVER-UP

In the aftermath of Israel's lies and heinous behavior, Senator Barry Goldwater and Adlai Stevenson both called for full investigations, while a secret 1976 congressional inquiry report concluded that Israel's attack upon the *Liberty* had been deliberate. In addition, a recent Independent Commission of Inquiry declared that Israel had committed "an act of war" against the U.S. Captain Ward Boston, chief legal counsel for the board of inquiry, some 35 years after the attack in a signed affidavit, even went so far as to say that Lyndon Johnson and Robert McNamara told those heading the initial naval inquiry (of which he was an integral part) to conclude that the attack was "a case of mistaken identity despite overwhelming evidence to the contrary."

Yet to this day, similar to the terrorist attacks on 9-11, no one has been held accountable, no one has stood up to take responsibility, and none of the guilty parties has been brought to justice. Why? What were LBJ and Robert McNamara trying to cover-up? By law, Lyndon Johnson knew he had to order an investigation into this attack. But he was mortally afraid that the public would learn about his orders *not* to save the *Liberty* by calling back aircraft that were already en route to rescue the American ship. Johnson's actions were so unforgivable that he actually uttered at one point, "I don't care how many Americans are killed. . . . I will not embarrass our ally."

Anyone who has read Michael Collins Piper's *Final Judgment* already knows what a lackey and subservient boot-licker LBJ was to the Jewish state; while a report in the *Spotlight* newspaper on November 21, 1977 pointed out that CIA counter-intelligence chief James J. Angleton also helped Israel in orchestrating this attack. In the end, LBJ brought in the ultimate Washington, D.C. fixer—and later BCCI bank fraud criminal—Clark Clifford to help smooth over this mess, then pawned off the investigation to a spineless Navy admiral named John S. McCain Jr., father of senator and presidential candidate John McCain.

PART FIVE—THE MCCAIN HEARINGS

Since the *USS Liberty* was attacked by Israel on June 8th, 1967, not once has a surviving *Liberty* crewman been allowed to testify in a court of law. Not only that, the one-and-only hearing presided over by Admiral Isaac Kidd, was held in secret, the press was barred from attendance, and every sailor and communications technician aboard the ship was told they would be court-martialed if they ever spoke a word about what had happened. The government's cover-up was so heavy-handed that military officers even imprisoned certain sailors against their will in psychiatric wards, drugged them and threatened them with electroshock to keep them from speaking.

The first *USS Liberty* hearings were overseen by Admiral Kidd, operating under orders of Admiral John S. McCain Jr., who was the European commander-in-chief of the U.S. Navy. Despite the seriousness of these attacks, Admiral McCain only gave his investigators one week to gather evidence.

But the loathsome behavior of admirals McCain and Kidd didn't end there, as sailors who went against the official "party line" were ordered to "shut up; we don't want to hear that. If you ever tell the truth you'll be court-martialed and spend the rest of your life in a military prison at Fort Leavenworth."

Even more peculiar, it was later discovered that on June 6th, 1967—two days before the *Liberty*'s attack—the Joint Chiefs of Staff sent Captain McGonagle an urgent message telling him to move the *Liberty* at least a hundred miles off the Gaza coast. But somehow *Liberty* never got the message. Why?

To implicate himself even further, Admiral McCain's instructions to Admiral Kidd prior to the hearings demanded protecting Israel's reputation! As an aside, one question must be asked: whatever happened to bringing the guilty parties to justice?

With these ground rules firmly in place, even though admirals McCain and Kidd believed *with certainty* that Israel's attack on the *Liberty* was deliberate—and that the Israeli pilots involved, as well as their superiors, knew it was an American ship—they still ruled it a case of mistaken identity.

Admiral McCain ultimately approved these conclusions even though Captain Merlin Staring, a Navy legal officer, who later became judge advocate—the highest legal officer in the U.S. Navy—said the 700-page report was flawed, incomplete, and contrary to the evidence. Worse, to prevent these men from speaking to any news organizations, Admiral Kidd, under McCain's direction, placed every surviving crewman under a permanent gag order.

Years later, Arizona Senator John McCain, son of the aforementioned Admiral John McCain, penned a biography entitled *Faith of My Fathers*. On the book jacket it said, "John McCain learned about life and honor from his grandfather and father, both four-star admirals in the U.S. Navy. This is a memoir about their lives, their heroism, and the ways that sons are shaped and enriched by their fathers."

A fair question every American has the right to ask is this: Senator McCain, what kind of honor is found in betraying your country? What kind of honor is found in selling-out the lives of those sailors who died aboard the *USS Liberty*? And Senator McCain, what kind of heroism is shaped from covering-up this matter for over forty years? The only kind of honor and heroism that you—an influential U.S. senator—can display right now is by immediately re-opening this investigation and shining a bright light of justice on those guilty parties who acted so reprehensibly and were responsible for this tragic, sickening event.

PART SIX—ISRAEL'S MOTIVES

At this point, the foremost question on everyone's mind should be: What were Israel's motives in attacking the *USS Liberty*? Answers will be provided throughout this book, but first, please remember that the Israeli leaders at that time only "admitted their mistake" when they were caught red-handed, after the fact. Only then did they come up with a cock-n-bull story that the attacks were due to "mistaken identity."

So, what were Israel's motives? First and foremost, Israel attacked the *USS Liberty* and absolutely tried to leave no survivors and no trace of responsibility because they wanted to blame it on the Egyptians, thus drawing America into the Six Day War on Israel's side. Such a scenario is especially pertinent today, particularly when looked at in light of Israel's many ties to the 9-11 terrorist attacks, the present wars in Iraq and Afghanistan, and the fact that Israel's primary objective has been, and always will be, the primacy of the Jewish state.

Another likely motive is the fact that Israel's U.S. ambassador, Avraham Harmon, assured President Lyndon Johnson that Israel would not attack Syria during the Six Day War. But the Israelis had already amassed troops along the West Bank and Golan Heights, and were primed for further invasions.

But with the *USS Liberty* positioned off the Sinai Peninsula, it would be readily able to send back reports that Israel had indeed lied and violated their agreement. Thus, similar to their sneak attack on the Egyptians in starting the Six Day War (whose fighter jets were still parked on the runway), the Israelis could only engage in a similar attack on Syria after they Pearl Harbored the *USS Liberty* and removed it from the picture

Lastly, on the very day the *Liberty* was attacked, the Israeli Defense Forces under the command of Ariel "Bulldozer" Sharon was in the process of slaughtering and executing at least a thousand Egyptian and Palestinian prisoners of war, and then burying them beneath the sands of the Sinai Desert. Israeli army officers admitted to this massacre years later—a clear and undeniable example of yet another war crime committed by the Jewish state. The *Liberty* would have picked up radio transmissions proving this war crime, something that Israel preferred not be made public.

PART SEVEN—CONCLUSION

In the end, we need to ask ourselves: Why does the state of Israel hold such a diabolical, hypnotic sway over the United States? After bombing the *USS Liberty* on June 8th, 1967, were the Israeli leaders apologetic for their heinous actions? Hardly. Instead, they called the sailors who tried to reveal the truth about what happened to them "anti-Semites" and "Jew haters."

Even worse, why is the very government tasked with protecting the American people acting in the same way? The last country that initiated a similar act of war against the U.S. had two of its cities incinerated with nuclear weapons, a precedent that Lyndon Johnson obviously intended to repeat when he dispatched nuclear weapons-laden bombers toward the ancient city of Cairo under the "assumption" it was Egypt responsible for attacking the *Liberty*. Only when it was learned that indeed the *USS Liberty* had not yet sunk were bombers recalled and Israel was allowed to further pummel the defenseless American ship.

This indisputable act of treason committed by Lyndon Johnson and Robert McNamara—and the subsequent kangaroo court cover-up hearings conducted by Admiral John McCain—were clearly an obstruction of justice to an incalculable degree.

With all this in mind, one gnawing question needs to be asked: Why is it that members of the U.S. government were more concerned with covering for Israel, especially after being caught red-handed bombing the *USS Liberty*, than they are in getting justice for the families of those who were brutally killed? Why weren't the guilty parties brought to trial and convicted of war crimes? And finally, why hasn't the Israeli government been publicly told in no uncertain terms to never ever again kill an American citizen?

This sickening display of raw hatred for America did not end in the days and weeks following the attack and so-called "investigation." Consider the case of Grafton, Wisconsin, where a library was built in honor of the *USS Liberty*. Instead of applauding this patriotic effort, Jewish groups campaigned to label the town as "anti-Semitic," while the U.S. government demanded that no Navy personnel be allowed to attend the ceremony. Death threats were hurled at those responsible for funding the library, and on the day it was ceremonially dedicated, SWAT teams were deployed on rooftops to fend off any violent attacks by Jewish interests—in America, *the land of the free and home of the brave*. Truly despicable behavior if ever there was any.

After Israel blatantly betrayed America by attacking the *Liberty*, how much financial aid did Uncle Sam cut off to them? The answer: none. Not a red cent, not a thin dime. Despite the fact that Israel is the world's sixteenth wealthiest nation and accounts for a measly one-tenth of one-percent of the world's total population, they still receive over one-third of all U.S. foreign aid. In fact, in 1997 alone, the total amount of U.S. grants and loan guarantees to Israel, plus the interest costs associated with these payments, came to a whopping 8.7 billion dollars! That translates to nearly $24 million a day—ONE MILLION DOLLARS AN HOUR—every day, 7 days a week, 365 days a year.

Furthermore, the U.S. Congress has forgiven every single loan ever made to Israel and dropped the entire cost of both principal and interest in the lap of the American taxpayers. Showing just how much the Jewish state "feels America's pain" in 2002, a year of great economic turmoil in the U.S., where millions of U.S. workers were losing jobs and when deficits soared through the roof, Israel had the audacity to ask (demand) another $14 billion in annual aid, or in other words, $38 million a day.

The first step in dealing with what was done to the *USS Liberty* is to expose the following men for their part in the attack and subsequent cover-up: Moshe Dayan, Lyndon Johnson, Robert McNamara, John S. McCain Jr., and Ariel Sharon. These individuals are war criminals, traitors, and are guilty of treason and war crimes. The pages of history should remember and recount their barbaric behavior.

The next step is obvious: public, full-disclosure hearings to set the record straight instead of sidling up to the Israeli government and covering up their sordid actions. To begin this process, we are reminded of some very powerful words spoken by Admiral Thomas Moorer, who said that to get at the truth, Congress must first overcome its fear of the pro-Israeli lobby.

The contributors to this book can't think of any truer words.

—VICTOR THORN, updated June 2009

Survivor Stories

Overviews Written by Victor Thorn

LARRY WEAVER: "Ship Without a Country"

"On June 8, 1967, the *USS Liberty* became a ship without a country, and has been a ship without a country ever since." These sad, yet powerful words originated from a man who's spent decades haunted by tragic memories.

As a 21-year-old crewman working as a lookout on the ship's bow, Larry Weaver's patrol duties took him to the catwalk when an event began to unfold that would forever change his life. In the distance, Weaver observed a high-speed aircraft make two passes over his ship, its proximity so close that it nearly hit the *Liberty*'s mast.

Describing this first plane as a "dark gray flying boxcar," he next witnessed what he called "an old bucket of bolts" that had the Star of David emblazoned on its side. This aircraft approached the ship so closely that Weaver saw the pilot smiling, as well as the brightness of his teeth.

Initially, Weaver didn't feel concerned that these planes were any danger to his ship because, even though the Six Day War was being waged, Israel was supposedly America's ally and was looking out for her. More importantly, a huge American flag flapped in the wind above their ship, clearly visible to any oncoming pilots.

Weaver's first impressions were suddenly obliterated when a rocket blast shattered his body. Blown five feet in the air, he landed back on the deck, blood surrounding him everywhere. Critically wounded, he lay down, hoping to find safety. That's when the fallen seaman helplessly watched as an Israeli pilot saw him and deliberately dove in his direction.

The horrors continued, and despite his own injuries, Weaver pushed a fellow crewman out of the line of fire in order to save his life. Another man wasn't so lucky. Weaver looked on as the sailor's body was cut in half by the strafe.

In Weaver's opinion, these attacks were most certainly well calculated, and by no means accidental or a case of "mistaken identity." First, jet fighters with rockets and cannon fire riddled the ship with armor piercing munitions. Next came torrents of napalm, which burned the ship from within and without. Finally, gunboats unleashed volleys of torpedo fire.

As this unprovoked assault continued, the last thing Weaver noticed was a very large American flag above his head; the second one put in place after Israeli pilots shot down the first. Seriously injured, medics eventually dragged him to safety, only to find his abdominal area was on fire from the napalm. As doctors stuffed gauze into his wounds to stop the bleeding, another Israeli rocket burst through the ceiling, hitting the physician and wounding Weaver yet again.

Understandably, few expected Weaver to survive. With over 100 shrapnel wounds (60 shards remain within him today), he also lost a three-foot section of colon, has had both knees replaced, required a stainless steel left shoulder, and needed a one-foot-by-one-foot section of mesh to hold his abdominal cavity together.

Notwithstanding the trauma and physical pain, when Weaver got out of intensive care back in Philadelphia, officials summoned him to a small room, whereupon he met three-star Admiral Isaac Kidd. The admiral sat alongside Weaver, removed his stars, and then wanted to be told everything that the young crewman knew. After hearing his story, Kidd threatened him with imprisonment and said he'd lose the key if he ever mentioned these events to anyone.

To his amazement, Weaver said that he was "treated like a criminal by the U.S. government," and was told that he'd be abandoned in a federal prison if he ever spoke out. Further, all records pertaining to his duty aboard the *USS Liberty* were expunged, erased inside an Orwellian memory hole.

The indignities didn't end there. Although military personnel never informed him of his right to obtain VA benefits, once he did discover this avenue, a bureaucratic nightmare unfolded before him. Here was a man whom doctors aboard the *Liberty* told had one more hour to live if additional medical care wasn't provided. Then, for the next 29 years, he had to battle the VA in order for them to admit that his injuries were permanent.

Fortunately, there were a few men who acted honorably. Captain William McGonagle refused to leave the bridge while the attacks occurred until help arrived. When awarding McGonagle the Congressional Medal of Honor, the U.S. Navy first asked the Israeli government if they were allowed to present it to him. When granted permission, the ceremony took place in a remote naval shipyard rather than in the Oval Office, as is customary.

Despite the heroism shown toward his country and crew, those who should have been tried for treason relegated McGonagle's shining moment to the shadows, precisely the way they had with the *Liberty* itself. Two others seeking justice were Joint Chiefs Chairman Admiral Thomas Moorer and Secretary of State Dean Rusk, both of whom requested (unsuccessfully) an official investigation.

Obviously, Israeli officials refused to admit the attack was premeditated, and instead pleaded "mistaken identity." But, as Larry Weaver professes, "I know in my heart it was deliberate."

Regarding possible motives, Weaver postulates that the *USS Liberty*—floating legally in international waters—became a guinea pig, a sitting duck. Israel, engrossed in the Six Day War, attacked their ship in the hopes of blaming it on Egypt, which would have naturally drawn America into this conflagration. From Weaver's perspective, one of the men who coordinated this murderous act was Moshe Dayan, Israel's defense minister.

As a result of the war, Israel would obtain more land, and then receive twenty-three new fighter jets from the U.S. after their victory over Egypt.

When asked about his thoughts today, Weaver sums it up as such. "There's a difference between right and wrong, and what the U.S. government does 90% of the time doesn't represent what the average American feels or does." If every U.S. citizen were fully aware of what Israel did to our men that day, they would undoubtedly concur with Larry Weaver's profound assessment.

—Interview originally conducted for WING TV
by Victor Thorn & Lisa Guliani, January 26, 2005

JIM ENNES: "We Were Abandoned"

"We weren't defended at all. We were abandoned when we needed their help the most." Speaking of President Lyndon Baines Johnson, Admiral Kidd, and Defense Secretary Robert McNamara, *Assault on the Liberty* author Jim Ennes characterized the actions of these three men as "certainly treasonous." His assertions are frighteningly accurate because U.S. law requires that troops under attack will be protected and defended by the U.S. government. Yet when the Sixth Fleet attempted to intervene on the *Liberty*'s behalf, Johnson and McNamara were responsible for calling back the fighter planes.

Remembering that warm June summer day in 1967, Ennes served as the officer on deck from 8: am to 12 noon, then was back on the bridge from 1-2 pm. Prior to Israel's attack on their ship, they engaged in as many as 13 over-flights. At first unconcerned by these flyovers, Ennes walked up to the signal bridge (the *Liberty*'s highest point) and considered snapping a few pictures of the planes.

Then, without provocation, the shooting began and everyone on board hit the deck. Ennes contends that Israel's intent that day was to absolutely leave no survivors. He backs up this claim with references to transcripts from Israeli intercept operators, who told their pilots:

"Hit that ship and get out of there quickly."

"But sir, it's an American ship."

"Never mind, hit her."

Compounding this point, Ennes relates the details of a phone call he received after his book came out from an Israeli pilot on duty that afternoon. After recognizing an American flag atop the *Liberty*, he told his commander that he refused to attack, then returned to base. As a consequence for not following orders to bomb an American ship, the pilot was arrested, then discharged for bad conduct.

This failed mission proved to be a monumental embarrassment to Israel, as the intercept operators' sworn affidavits show. Listening to conversations between pilots and Israeli headquarters, they illustrate how military commanders were "hysterical because they couldn't sink the ship."

Conversely, even after the gunfire commenced, Ennes didn't suspect that Israeli planes were targeting the *Liberty*. Instead, he thought,

"Why are we shooting at them?" Then, after seeing flames originating from under the wings of incoming Israeli jets, he realized the *Liberty* was being attacked.

All remaining doubt quickly dissipated when a series of actions reflected Israel's true intent. For starters, the use of heat-seeking missiles proved premeditation. Furthermore, one of the first targets debilitated by the fighter jets were the *Liberty*'s outgoing communications transmitters. Considering that close to half a dozen of them were deliberately jammed, it points to clear foreknowledge of the frequencies being emitted. Miraculously, during bouts of intense gunfire, crewmen climbed the towers and hung wires to send an SOS signal.

Although referring to their grievous acts as a "tragic mistake," Israel's post-attack deception could not be more blatant. Ennes tells how eyewitnesses described lifeboats being machine-gunned by Israeli military personnel after examining them at close range. Further, one of these life rafts marked "U.S. Navy" was pulled on board an Israeli vessel, not to mention the *Liberty*'s name being clearly marked on the ship's stern, as well as a huge 7-foot-by-13-foot flag.

Unconscionably, IDF pilots and boatmen fired on anything that moved. The machine-gunning of life rafts constitutes a clear war crimes violation. This concept is crucial because even if Israel completely acted under the premise of mistaken identity, Ennes reminds everyone that the Geneva Convention still considers it a war crime to attack an unknown ship, even if it may be your opponent.

But let's not minimize this incident. On June 8, 1967, Israel viewed the *USS Liberty* and its crew as undeniable enemies. Allies don't blast six- and eight-foot holes in the side of a vessel, then douse it with napalm, which sloshed down through the gaping holes. Ennes described this gruesome process. "The military purpose of napalm, which is jellied flaming gasoline, is to destroy personnel. It ensures the destruction of troops, is lethal to ships, and turned the

Liberty into an inferno. Plus, there were two 55-gallon drums of gasoline on the port side of our ship. It was nasty that day."

Looking back, Ennes is incensed by the lack of response by his superiors. In his words, "The Navy failed to protect us." His crew was assured that if the *Liberty* got into any trouble, they'd have an aircraft there in ten minutes. To the Navy's credit, they did launch two different fighters seven minutes apart, only to have both called back on orders from Washington. Then, to cover up Israel's direct involvement, Ennes discovered years later that his logbook had been altered and rewritten before being sent to naval headquarters, with all mention of Israeli reconnaissance removed.

Considering the deaths, injuries and damage, the *USS Liberty* is the only U.S. naval vessel attacked in peacetime that didn't receive a full congressional investigation. In fact, not one member of Congress is willing to ask any questions because "it's too politically sensitive to investigate."

Mainstream media sources have not offered any consolation either. Ennes wonders why major news shows like *60 Minutes* have totally ignored their plight, while the networks never showed any sustained attention to this tragic tale. Thankfully, Ennes agrees that the *Spotlight* and *American Free Press* are two publications that have kept their story alive from the late 1960s to today. He also gives a nod to Admiral Thomas Moorer, who complimented him on the publication of his book.

In all, however, it's still a bitter pill for Ennes to swallow when thinking back on what he was told by Navy superiors: *"If you ever speak about this incident, we'll put you in jail."*

—Interview originally conducted for WING TV
by Victor Thorn & Lisa Guliani, January 27, 2005

DAVE LEWIS: It Was a War Crime

Although too frequently overused nowadays, the word "hero" certainly applies to Dave Lewis, an officer in charge of the *Liberty*'s Research Department. As Israeli bombs pummeled the U.S. Navy spy ship, Lewis experienced an excruciating amount of physical pain. Burnt paint was thrust into his eyes; the resulting damage so severe that doctors lanced his eyelids and scraped the burnt paint off his eyeballs. Temporarily blinded, he also suffered severe damage to his eardrums, while a piece of concrete pierced his lip as shrapnel wracked all parts of his body.

Obviously traumatized by this unexpected onslaught, years later Lewis tells an amusing story of what happened next. When help finally arrived many hours later, the most severely wounded were hoisted from the *Liberty* to a helicopter, which flew them to the *USS America*. Wrapped in bandages from head-to-toe, Lewis was strapped into a basket and lifted into the helicopter. However, during this frantic emergency flight, a crewman couldn't differentiate Lewis' head from his toes, so he sat directly on his head! Lewis laughed, "What an ignominious way to die, especially after surviving a torpedo attack."

Others didn't fare as well, and the resulting casualties were particularly painful to Lewis. Of the 34 men who died aboard the *Liberty*, 28 worked for him. Worse, two were eligible for retirement, yet were asked to deploy for one final mission. Both died at their posts. These men were part of the *Liberty*'s intel collecting division, and as such worked in what became known as "The Secret Place" under direct command of the NSA (National Security Agency).

Of special interest on an epic scale were sealed orders contained in the *Liberty*'s safe regarding "Operation Cyanide." Of the 200+ personnel aboard this ship, Lewis was only one of two people cleared to open a safe containing sealed letters. When asked about the type of information contained in these documents, Lewis replied, "In the event of hostilities, we were to open them [the sealed letters] and it would authorize communication via submarines." He continued, "If the bombs went up, all HF communications would have been obliterated and nuclear weapons would have then taken off into the ionosphere."

Undoubtedly, the subject being broached is of the highest importance, as Lewis said matter-of-factly. "If launched, we would have been three minutes away from nuclear war. We were certainly closer that day than at any time during the Cuban Missile Crisis."

With heightened tensions in the Middle East surrounding the Six Day War, Israel's attack on the *Liberty* was perilously risky; and, according to Lewis, "most deliberate." As proof, he points to Israeli Major Seth Mintz, who worked in a Tel Aviv war room and said everyone present knew their jet fighters were attacking an American ship. Likewise, pilot Evan Toni immediately recognized the *Liberty* as belonging to the U.S.

Lewis described the attack as "certainly brutal and in violation of the Geneva Convention ... a war crime." Considering the technical responsibilities of his job, Lewis suspected the use of heat-seeking missiles on Israel's behalf because they immediately targeted the tuning section of the *Liberty*'s HF antennas, which generate plenty of heat. With their communications network disabled, Lewis describes how they survived. "The only reason we got an SOS out was because our crazy troops were climbing antennas and stringing long wires while the attacks were taking place."

Conventional wisdom holds that the *USS Liberty* sat alone in international waters during the siege; but was an EC-21 (and even a U.S. submarine) in the vicinity? Although NSA officials deny it, Lewis claims that a navigator and intercept operator both confirmed they were monitoring the assault as it proceeded.

If this scenario is accurate, how did news of this event spread to the highest channels of our government? Lewis asserts that none other than James Jesus Angleton—director of the CIA's Counterintelligence Division—notified Lyndon Johnson, who then contacted Robert McNamara. Considering Angleton's unabashed allegiance to Israel and how he's regarded as a hero there, it seems reasonable that this superspook would intervene to protect them. Subsequently, LBJ uttered his now infamous remark about Israel: "I will not embarrass an ally."

Lewis also suggests that the Office of Naval Intelligence participated in the cover-up at the highest and lowest levels, while no sooner had he opened his eyes than he was escorted into the office of Rear Admiral Lawrence Geis, who swore him to secrecy. He also discovered Robert McNamara's betrayal in recalling fighter jets on two different occasions.

Even though ample information has surfaced over the years proving Israel's premeditation, including Moshe Dayan's ultimate responsibility for ordering the attacks, an arrogant defiance still persists among many in the IDF. For example, Mirage pilot and Brigadier General Yiftah Spector incredulously sneered, *"As far as I know, the mistake was on the USS Liberty for being there in the first place."* Closer to home, when crewmen realized the potential danger facing them and requested an escort destroyer to accompany them into these hostile waters, Admiral William Martin denied them.

Liberty survivors didn't receive any more help in Washington, either. Lewis sums up their reactions. "Politicians worry about votes, and votes depend on where the money comes from. There's a lot of money that comes from pro-Zionist forces. If anyone speaks negatively about Israel, they're instantly labeled anti-Semitic."

One of the primary figures to turn his back on the *Liberty* by covering up these war crimes was Admiral John McCain, Jr., father of Arizona Senator John McCain. Years later, Lewis contacted the Arizona senator and presidential candidate and asked if he'd investigate this matter. McCain said he'd consider it if any new information surfaced. Lewis handed him three large packets of data, yet never heard another word from McCain. Like father, like son. Captain William McGonagle also sent letters to Bill Clinton and George W. Bush asking them to convene a presidential panel. Both ignored his plea.

As with other *Liberty* crewmembers, Dave Lewis also recognizes some good guys who tried to help their cause. In addition to Admiral Moorer and Dean Rusk, he tips his hat to senators Barry Goldwater, Adlai Stephenson, and Pete McCloskey, all of who wanted an open inquiry.

As the years and decades pass without any justice, Lewis maintains himself by valiantly asking, "What can I do to vindicate the lives of our fallen soldiers who died on the *USS Liberty*?"

—Interview originally conducted for WING TV
by Victor Thorn & Lisa Guliani, January 28, 2005

ERNIE GALLO: "Don't Let Them Die for Nothing"

Electrical technician Ernie Gallo will never forget his fallen brothers. "34 men were murdered by the Israelis, and we're not going to let them die for nothing. Even if the media won't tell you the truth about it, we will. You don't spend two hours strafing and bombing a ship that you don't intend to sink."

Truer words could not be spoken, for over 800 holes ended up being blasted through the *USS Liberty*. Quite literally, plenty of miracles occurred that day to keep this ship from sinking. Consider that a 40-foot-by-30-foot hole was torn in the ship's side. But, incredibly, the torpedo that penetrated its exterior and created this damage hit in the one and only place that allowed it to stay afloat. An inch to the left or right would have meant certain demise for the vessel.

Another factor in the *Liberty*'s favor involved its history. Initially a converted cargo ship constructed during WW II, Gallo says proudly, "It was very well built. The *Liberty* took one heck of a lot of punishment."

One of his fellow crewmates, John Hrankowski, was working in the engine room when the torpedo assault began. This area was a much more vulnerable place for something to happen, especially when the Israelis fired armor-piercing .50 caliber machine gun shells, that tore through the ship's skin. Hrankowski said without hesitation that the Israelis were intent on exploding the boiler, and most certainly knew what they were doing by targeting that room.

This anecdote told by a survivor leads us once again to the issue of premeditation. Ernie Gallo recalls that serene day when his ship floated in the Mediterranean Sea. While on duty, his captain called a few men over and pointed into the distance, where they saw smoke and fire. The Six Day War still raged, and their superior wanted to instill in them that this situation should be taken very seriously.

Being lawfully afloat in international waters, the men didn't feel threatened or alarmed. At one point, Gallo went below deck, grabbed a Coke, and then heard a tremendous grinding noise emanating from the topside. At first he thought an engine of some sort had gone bad. But once incoming fighter jets began strafing their ship with gunfire, followed later by torpedo boats, that's when the brutal realization of this attack hit home.

Gallo confided, "It was incredible to see what the ship had gone through—holes in the walls like peeled paper. It's a miracle that anyone survived. It's hard to imagine the amount of damage and destruction. The helm was completely blown away." He paused; then continued succinctly. "Incredible carnage … bodies." In all, he witnessed 25 corpses, many of them coated in oil because torpedo fire had ruptured their fuel tanks. "The scene was horrific. You can't imagine what it looked like."

As to the question of whether this event could have been a case of mistaken identity, Gallo's response is firm and simple—"no." The reason why is because this Navy ship had some of the most unique antennas conceivable. One sixteen-foot dish mounted on a pedestal couldn't be missed due to its configuration. There were other dishes and antennas used for radar, with one that looked like a Christmas tree. Gallo summarized it thusly: "The *Liberty* could not have been mistaken for anything other than a communications ship."

One must keep in mind that the *Liberty* was a spy ship used for surveillance, and once the attack commenced, Gallo recalls picking up scattered classified materials and placing them in bags. These were some of the memories he and other survivors spoke about many years later, characterized as a "healing process." Gallo and his crewmates often returned to that tragic day to discuss the minutest of details. Such meetings didn't result for decades, though, because after the assault on June 8, 1967, *Liberty* crewmen were scattered and sent on different assignments while being monitored, watched, and threatened.

One element of the attack that ironically proved beneficial involved the arrival of Israeli helicopters, which followed the fighter jets and torpedo boats. Seeing that the *Liberty* had not been sunk, these helicopters had "hostile intentions." But, unexpectedly, they were called off. Why? The answer lies in the fact that after the Sixth Fleet launched a squadron of rescue planes, the Israelis intercepted this message and got scared. Not wanting an air battle with U.S. forces, they retreated. For whatever reason, they didn't hear LBJ's subsequent recall command, so the helicopters never had a chance to finish the job.

Understandably, the betrayal by our government still stings Mr.

Gallo; but to his credit, he's not bitter at the country or military as a whole. "It's very difficult for me to condemn the entire system when I've encountered so many other fine Americans whose hearts are in the right place. The American public needs to know the truth."

Gallo harbors no doubt that the orders for this cover-up originated from those above his Navy commanders. He instead squarely places blame for the conspiracy on Lyndon Johnson, Robert McNamara, and the nation of Israel. As a protest to one of the most shameful chapters in American history, Gallo refused to attend the award ceremony where Captain William McGonagle received his Congressional Medal of Honor. He felt it was disgraceful that instead of immediately being presented by President Lyndon Johnson at the White House, the function took place years later at a remote Navy yard, with an undersecretary overseeing the function. Gallo likened this obvious slight as "indicative of President Johnson's mindset."

Upset and disappointed by these betrayals, Gallo receives solace from Admiral Thomas Moorer. "At least he believed in us." He then quotes a line from Moorer that encapsulates the entire sordid affair. "If this had been written as fiction, nobody would believe it."

—Interview originally conducted for WING TV
by Victor Thorn & Lisa Guliani, February 18, 2005

ADM. MERLIN STARING: "Shocked and Chagrined"

"If the true facts of this attack in 1967, plus the nature and quality of the investigation, were widely known, any reasonable person would know this is not the way to treat sailors and men from the armed forces who are serving their country."

When Rear Admiral Merlin Staring speaks, people should listen. As a former judge advocate general in the U.S. Navy, as well as treasurer of the USS LIBERTY ASSOCIATION, he has become an outspoken, tireless champion of truth. He was one of the first men to witness the official written record from the Navy court of inquiry regarding the *Liberty* attack. Delivered to him by Captain Ward Boston on June 17, 1967, Staring studied nearly half of this 600+ page document, only to have Boston reappear 18 hours later and retake possession of it. Why did this emissary for the Navy Court of Inquiry not allow Staring to finish his work?

Staring answers emphatically. "The report was terribly flawed. I was shocked and chagrined to cosmetically find it a poor piece of work. There were typographical errors, incorrect citations, and it lacked credibility."

Contradicting official claims that "numerous investigations" have been carried out over the years, Representative Rob Simmons made an appeal to the Department of Navy in March, 2005 and discovered that the Navy court of inquiry only looked into this matter one time, in 1967. This was the *only* investigation of the *USS Liberty* attack ever conducted by the U.S. government.

Obviously not satisfied with their contrived results or constant excuses that this matter was "old hat," Admiral Thomas Moorer, General Raymond G. Davis (USMC), Staring, and Ambassador James Akins released their own independent commission report in 2003. What conclusions did they reach? "The results are so damning and conclusive," Staring says strongly, "that we can't understand how the government continues denying it. There was a deliberate cover-up. During the initial investigation, they shortcut the proceedings and squelched any comments that were inconsistent with what was delivered to them via diplomatic channels. It was a criminal and dastardly cover-up."

Not everyone in official circles accepted these grotesque lies. U.S. Secretary of State Dean Rusk communicated to the Israeli government that their attack on an American ship must be condemned as an act of military irresponsibility. He added that provisions exist to prevent the use of deadly force against a neutral vessel, even if by "mistake."

Admiral Staring's assessment is not quite so conciliatory. "There was no legitimate reason to attack a neutral vessel of the United States. It was totally unjustified, and as such qualified as an act of war." His opinions carry over to the recall of military support dispatched by the U.S. Navy's Sixth Fleet. Had they been permitted to intervene, Israel's torpedo attacks would not have occurred, and most certainly the lives of 25 men would have been spared. Even more inexcusably, Israeli pilots deliberately shot at firefighters, rescuers on the ship's deck, and the wounded who lay there bleeding. Again, Staring stresses, Israel is guilty of war crimes, and "these facts have been concealed from the public and history."

Unwilling to remain silent, on June 8, 2005, Staring delivered a ten-page letter compiled by the Liberty Veterans Association to U.S. Navy Admiral Mark Hill. This report detailing Israel's war crimes similarly reached the secretary of the Army. Survivors have also communicated with, petitioned, and written to Congress, not to mention Senator John McCain. Despite being part of the cover-up, McCain's father did concede that the *USS Liberty* suffered an unprovoked attack by Israeli air and naval forces in international waters. To date, none of these representatives conveyed any indication or disposition to reopen the case.

Staring is grateful that a few silver linings do exist. Although the original cover-up kept most men in the dark circa 1967, due to their uncompromising efforts, "there is a great deal of appreciation by personnel of the Navy who've learned the true facts. I'm sure they're incensed by what occurred," Staring says assuredly.

Secondly, he gives a touching account of his close friend, Admiral Thomas Moorer, who, even on his deathbed, kept asking about Dr. Tito Howard, Staring, and the LIBERTY VETERANS ASSOCIATION. Moreover, despite mainstream media sources refusing to mention Moorer's affiliation with the *USS Liberty*, at least he received a fitting and lengthy tribute at his funeral. Such recognition ensures that the *Liberty* and its crew will not be forgotten.

—Interview originally conducted for WING TV
by Victor Thorn & Lisa Guliani, December 12, 2005

JOE LENTINI: "It Wasn't a Mistake"

Indicative of how surviving *Liberty* crewmembers have been treated over the years, Joe Lentini tells a heartbreaking story of the ultimate disgrace. When Captain William McGonagle received his Congressional Medal of Honor, insult was added to injury. Not only were the ceremonies relegated to a back room at the Naval shipyard (overseen by an under secretary of defense), he and his fellow shipmates were then snubbed at the White House.

Following the award presentation, a meeting had been arranged for McGonagle to meet President George Bush, Sr. The men stood outside in the garden for several hours—McGonagle in full regalia with his medals—until two presidential limousines drove past. In the first, President Bush rolled down his window and waved as they continued through a back gate. When the second arrived, aides John Sununu and Brent Scowcroft got out and told the forgotten heroes that President Bush didn't have enough time to take five minutes out of his schedule to shake their hands.

Humiliated, saddened, and once again betrayed, the *Liberty* contingent left without even a thank you. John Sununu later denied this meeting ever took place; but when media sources showed him a snapshot of the brief encounter, he quipped, "Oh, yeah, I must have forgot about it." Rumors have also filtered through the grapevine that a representative from the state of Israel awaited President Bush at the White House. He'd heard about the possible meeting with *Liberty* crewmembers and wanted to put an immediate stop to it.

Joe Lentini suffers now, and he suffered on June 8, 1967. During Israel's murderous rampage, he received a four-inch gash in his leg, a collapsed lung, broken ribs and a broken left leg, in addition to being knocked unconscious.

He's lucky to be alive, and the attack was most certainly not an accident. Lentini provides quite a number of reasons that substantiate this claim. For instance, visibility on that crystal clear day extended thirteen miles. The *Liberty*'s huge American flag flapped in the wind, and there could be no mistaking their vessel for that of any other. A converted World War II transport ship, its distinct antennas could be discerned miles away. Plus, prior to their brutal offensive, the state of Israel made a formal request to U.S. authorities to move their ship farther away from shore because *Israel wasn't sure they could protect them*! So, they had already positively identified the *Liberty*, and eight hours prior to the onslaught, their officers referred to it as a U.S. intelligence ship.

"Anyone who was on that ship, myself included," Lentini declares, "will tell you it wasn't a mistake. They blew out our topside hatches, hit our only gas tank, machine-gunned the life rafts, and took out our antennas. For them to hit these targets, each pilot would have had to be pre-briefed before the attack with photographs of the targets."

In the hours leading up to this bombing, slow-moving Israeli aircraft flew over the *Liberty*, clearly marked with the Star of David. Crewmembers snapped pictures, waved, and were waved back at by the pilots. A "photographer to the bridge" command was even ordered where pictures were taken of the planes.

When presented with this overwhelming evidence, detractors still persist. Two of the most egregious are Jay Cristol and Hank Roth, who've written that the attack was a case of "friendly" fire, and those who say otherwise "want to hurt Israel and demonize the Jewish people. . . . They're the kind of people who associate with crackpots, anti-Semites, and are in league with Holocaust deniers."

Lentini calls these smears "totally bogus," adding, "Their conclusions aren't backed up by documentation." When asked about Israel's intentions, he explains that they've done "similar things to the U.S. and other nations, including placing spies in our country. . . . Israel wanted to expand their borders, yet previous presidents wouldn't allow it. If they did so, financial support would have been pulled. Then LBJ had an opportunity to create a situation like the *USS Maine*. If Israel killed all the *Liberty* crewmen, our rallying cry would have been reminiscent of, 'Remember the *Maine*—blame the Arabs.'"

Referring to the Six Day War and how Israel expanded their borders to the Golan Heights, Lentini cites Moshe Dayan, who admitted that this war had nothing to do with Israeli security, but instead total greed. They wanted the land, profits, and produce of a "Greater Israel."

Regarding the cover-up, Lentini accurately describes how those who control our country's media and money are friendly with Israel, and that no politicians want to alienate them. They have dual allegiances, with Israel receiving preferential treatment. No more grave example could be provided than when President Johnson sneered that he'd rather "see our ship go to the bottom of the ocean than embarrass an ally."

Lentini also recalls a monumental meeting he had while recovering in the hospital. A submarine sailor admitted that as their ship floated in the Mediterranean off the Sinai Coast and was attacked without warning, they saw the entire episode from their sub. Lentini went on to add that it's not unusual to have this happen because military intelligence aircraft also recorded the attack on the *USS Pueblo* years before.

The pain from these memories still lingers, and Lentini will never forget how George Bush Sr. treated them at the White House. "No president ever had anything to do with the *Liberty* survivors. Even LBJ was advised to keep an arm's length away from the *Liberty* for political reasons."

—Interview originally conducted for WING TV
by Victor Thorn & Lisa Guliani, April 14, 2005

GARY BRUMMETT: "*Liberty* Attack Was No Accident"

"We all know Roosevelt allowed Pearl Harbor to take place, and we all know the Gulf of Tonkin story was some of Johnson's garbage. I hope I live long enough to see our government allow the information to come forward showing the *Liberty* attack was no accident."

Third class petty officer Gary Brummett has seen plenty of propaganda and misinformation since his days as a self-described "naïve 20-year-old" aboard the *Liberty*. Being one of the survivors, he tells how even after the onslaught, the U.S. government still played games.

With 800+ holes in their ship, instead of allowing it to dock at a closer port only two days away, the *Liberty* was forced to travel another 1,200 miles over five days. Eventually resting in Malta, Brummett confessed to being afraid to sleep in his rack because the ship had taken such a beating.

After finally reaching safe harbor on June 13, none of the men was permitted to leave dry dock or take shore leave until a Navy lieutenant and commander told them what to do and say. More precisely, they could not—under any circumstances—give interviews or speak to newsmen; nor could they let anyone know what happened on June 8th due to *national security reasons*. If they did talk, it would be considered a direct betrayal of the government.

During their arduous five-day trip to Malta, the crewmen discussed this horrid attack amongst themselves. None could figure out why a 455-foot ship weighing 10,000 tons clearly displaying an American flag atop its 125-foot mast would be attacked by Israel. Israeli pilots later said that smoke obscured the flag, but with wind gusts at twenty miles per hour, these statements are absolutely untrue.

One of Brummett's associates, U.S. Navy Officer Lloyd Painter, helped those who were injured to the main deck. As he went up to starboard and popped the hatch, Painter saw torpedo boats shooting up their life rafts. Brummett characterized Painter as a man with impeccable credentials: "I'd stake my life on what he says." Painter knew things weren't right that day, but after testifying at the one-and-only government investigation, crucial elements were excised out of the original report by Captain Ward Boston.

Isaac Kidd and Boston were the two men in charge of investigating the *Liberty* attack. Boston sat quiet for 35 years; then finally spoke out by revealing that he knew Israel's attack was intentional. In the four-plus decades since, seven or eight congressmen have tried to help the *Liberty* cause by opening a new investigation. Each suffered defeat in their next election and was unseated because millions of dollars were thrown to the opposing candidate.

One of the groups wielding so much power, money, and influence is AIPAC (America Israel Public Affairs Committee). This is why Congress is terrified to do anything that runs counter to the wishes of the Jewish state.

The latest casualty was Representative Cynthia McKinney, who called for an investigation into the attack on the *Liberty*. Like others before her, she lost her next re-election campaign. Brummett surmises that this hijacking of our government is why U.S. Middle East policy has completely failed.

Denied by the executive and legislative branches, Brummett also endured many years of what he calls "survivor's guilt." Stationed in the fire room when Israel commenced its onslaught, he stood between two boilers that became so thickened with smoke that he couldn't read his gauge board.

Then, when an announcement of "stand by for torpedo attack" echoed across the ship, Brummett felt death was imminent. Fourteen feet below sea level in the belly of this ship, "I thought I was fixing to die," he recalled, the reality of these memories still very much with him.

To his credit, he—like many others—is still keeping the flame alive. Referring to a War Crimes Report that would have to be moved through the judicial branch, Brummett insists this is the only way justice will ever be realized. The candle can never be extinguished, because what they've been fighting for transcends military duty, medals, and nation-states. "I'm trying to do what I'm doing for the guys who got killed," he said.

—Interview originally conducted for WING TV
by Victor Thorn & Lisa Guliani, January 11, 2006

Operation Cyanide

A Review of Peter Hounam's Book Explains How the *Liberty* Attack Almost Caused WWIII

BY VICTOR THORN

Officially classified as a "technical research ship," it must not be forgotten that the *USS Liberty*'s primary purpose revolved around spying. Such a status is key to understanding why it ultimately got attacked. Also referred to as a Sigint Collector (Signal Intelligence Collector), the National Security Group had 150 men in its employ on the *Liberty*, all of whom amassed intelligence data for the NSA. Specifically, in June, 1967 they monitored Israel's aggression against Egypt and Jordan during the Six Day War.

Claims that the inhuman massacre of Americans by Israeli forces was the result of "mistaken identity" are patently deceptive. Equipped only with four .50 caliber machine guns, the *Liberty* possessed virtually no ability to defend itself. Again, the picture here is of a spy ship with 45 aerials, a Moon-bounce dish, naval markings, and a huge, prominently displayed U.S. flag. There's not a military pilot anywhere who'd confuse it with an aged Egyptian freighter used to transport horses that was only one-quarter the *Liberty*'s size.

Far from accepting responsibility, some Israeli military men continued to blame the crew. Yet, their jets and torpedo boats came within fifty feet of the ship. Even afterward, when Admiral Isaac Kidd finished his report and forwarded it to Admiral John McCain, Jr., who then gave it his stamp of approval, the verdict left no doubt of a cover-up: "mistaken identity" indeed.

THE ATTACK

Israel's mission, quite simply, can be summarized in seven words: sink the ship and eliminate its crew. Try, they did. Fifteen different fighter jets targeted the *Liberty*, and along with naval forces, they pummeled the ship with more than 800 rocket hits. During their initial strikes, IDF pilots zeroed-in on American sailors on deck, riddling their bodies with bullets and "throwing them in the air like rag dolls." When crewmembers tried to escape, their rubber life rafts were machine-gunned. Or, equally as sickening, canisters of jellied petroleum (i.e. napalm) blanketed the deck and burst into flames. Radioman Gerald Surette called it "the most beat-up ship I ever saw afloat."

Peter Hounam writes, "The *Liberty* was the victim of a carefully planned and murderous attack in which the first move had been to wipe out its ability to reach the outside world." Such a contention is absolutely true, particularly when Israelis jammed the *Liberty*'s radio, including its international distress frequency. To do so, they had to have foreknowledge of the half-dozen frequencies used by the ship's shore-based receivers. This information was not acquired accidentally; and although no one has directly fingered him, the most likely culprit with access to such information would be CIA counterintelligence chief, James Jesus Angleton.

Valiantly, crewmen strung together a makeshift SOS system during the melee and were able to send a flash message to their CNO (chief naval officer). Upon receiving this distress signal, the Sixth Fleet notified Washington that the *Liberty* was under attack. In the meantime, Commander Lawrence Geis ordered the launching of aircraft to defend the helpless ship.

Joseph Tully, a captain aboard the *USS Saratoga*, revealed that 12 fighter-bombers and four tanker aircraft were immediately dispatched. While these planes were in route, President Lyndon Johnson called Robert McNamara and demanded that the rescue mission be aborted. Minutes later, Geis radioed Tully and told him to recall the planes. They repeated this exact procedure an hour later.

Hounam discloses some other highly explosive information. Flying high above the seas that day was an American EC-121 Ferret (Warning Star) designed to provide early warning of a nuclear attack. Obviously not wanting its murderous rampage to be monitored, the Israeli air force nearly shot this plane from the sky. Aboard the ship, Communications Technician Charles Rowley recalls photographing a large American flag only moments before the attack. Luckily for him, strafing bullets that swept across the deck hit his Nikon telephoto lens, smashing it to pieces, but saving his life in the process. Rowley's film was later confiscated by the Naval Court of Inquiry and stamped TOP SECRET.

Hounam delivers other astounding material, such as reports from Offutt Air Force Base in Omaha, Nebraska. In a highly secretive vault of the Strategic Air Command, sensitive signal communications from the National Security Agency (NSA) and other intelligence quarters were being handled. Monitoring the *Liberty*, these reports show the attack "was committed deliberately, with the intention of killing every single crewman. The Pentagon was aware of this from a very early stage, probably before Israeli planes opened fire."

These words are explosive, but the report continues. "Within minutes of the attack commencing, the Joint Chiefs knew it was Israel, and it is a mystery why they did nothing about it until the ship had been battered for an hour and a half."

Translating from the Hebrew, Offutt's report states, "It was imperative [the *USS Liberty*] be sunk quickly before it could alert American forces and get help. There could be no witnesses to the sinking."

All decisions for the IDF emanated from the Navy Command Center at Mount Carmel in Israel, with Captain Itzhak Rahav acting as the chief of naval operations.

In light of this revelation, military chief of staff Yitzhak Rabin selected Colonel Ram Ron to lead a one-man investigation. His conclusion: "It clearly appears that the American ship acted carelessly and placed herself in far-reaching peril ... without taking care to identify herself with conspicuous markings."

Even after admitting that helicopters carrying combat troops were dispatched to finish the job, Israel would still not come clean about its blatant complicity in this massacre.

THE SIX DAY WAR

Israeli officials weren't the only ones hiding the truth. While Defense Secretary Robert McNamara doesn't even mention the *Liberty* attack in his memoirs, it's now probable that White House records and timelines were altered to cover the fact that President Johnson was involved in this prearranged plot by Israel. On the other hand, one of the only men to show their contempt for this treasonous act was Dean Rusk. "I was never satisfied with the Israeli explanation. I didn't believe it then, and I don't believe it to this day."

If this attack had been determined beforehand, what occurred behind the scenes to bring it about? To contextualize this scenario, we must first understand that in June, 1967, the Israeli government had finally procured nuclear weapons at a facility in Dimona. They also initiated the Six Day War by attacking Egypt, with their sights also set on Jordan and occupied Palestinian territory.

By stealing even more land (again), they sought to realize their millennia-old dream of a Greater Israel. Lastly, Israel and the U.S. needed a pretext to strike against Egyptian President Gamal Abdel Nasser, who they viewed as a Soviet ally and the Middle East's most powerful Arab leader. From this perspective, LBJ and his cohorts must be seen as prime movers and initiators of the Six Day War, with the *USS Liberty* their ready-made excuse to help Israel finish the job in Egypt.

OPERATION CYANIDE

If LBJ directly conspired to set-up Israel's attack on the *Liberty*, the most obvious question is: why? It only takes one look at his cabinet to show where his loyalties lie.

- Walter Rostow—primary fixer
- Eugene Rostow—State Department
- Arthur Goldberg—U.N. ambassador
- Abe Fortas—Supreme Court associate justice
- Abraham Feinberg—Democratic fundraiser
- Leo White—White House counsel
- Jake Jacobsen—White House counsel
- Larry Levinson—White House aide

There are others, but this roster begins to explain why NSG duty officer Troy Hart declared, "Washington was informed that Israel was responsible in a signal from the *Liberty* within three or four minutes of the first distress message being identified."

But, if Israel knew the *Liberty*'s frequencies in order to jam them, a source must have existed. To uncover his identity, we need to look no further than Israeli General and Mossad director in 1967, Meir Amit. In the months preceding the Six Day War, Amit visited James Jesus Angleton in Washington to arrange U.S. coordination and cooperation for their offensive. Amit said boastfully, "I knew I could trust him [Angleton] like a brother."

Angleton didn't disappoint. As the head of CIA counterintelligence and controller of the agency's Israeli desk, he became a conduit for Amit. Awed by the Mossad's ability to penetrate his arch Cold War enemy—the Soviet Union—Angleton opened doors for Amit to Richard Helms at the CIA, plus Robert McNamara at the Pentagon. From there, none other than LBJ gave the green light to all that followed in the ensuing months.

What precisely did Operation Cyanide entail? According to Jim Sorrels of special operations, it was "a joint plan by elements of military intelligence in Israel and the United States to engineer a war with Egypt and depose [Egypt's] leader [Nasser] who, the U.S. believed, was a dangerous puppet of Moscow."

Amazingly, as this plot developed, the nuclear option became a definite consideration. Known as Condition November, after the *Liberty*'s attack, Admiral William Martin told crewmember Moe Shaffer that "four jets were on their way to Cairo loaded with nuclear weapons. He stated that we were three minutes from bombing them [the Egyptians]."

By law, the only individual authorized in the U.S. to launch a nuclear weapon is the president.

So, when Mike Ratigan, a catapult operator on the *USS America*, admitted that nuclear-armed Skyhawks were launched and only recalled three minutes before dropping their payload, the world spun perilously close to WW III. Condition November and American fighter jets with atomic bombs aboard them were a frightening reality on June 8, 1967. Johnson knew Russia would retaliate, for Soviet Premier Alexei Kosygin told him that if Israel or the U.S. initiated any type of further military offensive, they would assist the attacked country. The stage was set for full-fledged nuclear war.

303 COMMITTEE

Obviously, even James Jesus Angleton didn't have the sway to put a plan such as this into play. A higher authority needed to call the shots. Enter the 303 Committee, a secretive cabal within the Johnson cabinet that authorized various covert operations.

Also known as the "40 Committee" or the "Special Group," they became, in essence, a power unto themselves. On April 10, 1967, chairman (and fixer) Walt Rostow, Foy Kohler (deputy under secretary of State), and Admiral Rufus Taylor (CIA deputy chief) gave the OK to a sensitive Department of Defense SECRET—EYES ONLY project called Frontlet 615.

Hounam describes this operation as a "secret political agreement in 1966 by which Israel and the U.S. vowed to destroy Nasser. Operation Cyanide was the military name for putting it into effect."

The "615" aspect of this program purportedly came from when the Six Day War was intended to begin—June 15 (i.e. 615). So, not only did the 303 Committee examine covert operations and decide which ones to implement; they also provided President Johnson with plausible denial by removing him from direct involvement in black operations.

CONTACT X

We know this plan came to fruition for at least two different reasons. First of all, to prepare Israel for their attack on Egypt, from March to May 1967 the U.S. supplied the Jewish state with 400 tanks, 200 planes, jamming equipment and 1,000 military pilots. The second involved a secret agreement between Israel and American intelligence agencies where an American naval vessel would be attacked during the Six Day War.

But something intriguing happened along the way. Instead of simply limiting their expansionist aims to Egypt, Israel strayed from the game plan by faking phone calls from Nasser to Jordan's King Hussein.

Washington was already suspicious. The *Liberty* began picking up evidence of these compromising covert operations. In these faux phone calls, an Israeli impersonating Nasser said that Egypt's forces were reigning supreme, thus drawing Jordan into the battle to attain some of the spoils. Such a move would then allow Israel to attack Jordan and Syria, thereby letting them conquer even more land.

Because the *Liberty* intercepted these calls, they knew the truth about what transpired. In a case of *Spy vs. Spy*, Israel obviously didn't want anyone else to be made aware of these clandestine motives, so the *Liberty* had to be eliminated.

U.S. plotters from the 303 Committee are most assuredly not guilt-free either. Unbeknownst at the time to *Liberty* crewmembers was the positioning of a submarine almost directly beneath them that witnessed the entire attack, and possibly filmed it. Known as "Contact X," crewman Joe Lentini heard the following information from a soldier at the Portsmouth Naval Hospital in Virginia. "We were there in our submarine. We saw the whole thing. We took pictures. Then we sent an officer back to Washington to deliver them."

The submarine in question was the *US Amberjack SS522*, and those aboard it originally mistook Israel's onslaught as a depth charge attack because of the deafening gunfire, missiles, and torpedo explosions.

Then, to evade recognition, the submarine fled the scene without offering any assistance to the battered *Liberty*.

NUCLEAR WAR

One other variable distinguished the Contact X submarine from other vessels; namely, it was equipped with Polaris missiles armed with nuclear warheads. The *USS Liberty* had been deliberately sent into this hostile environment by LBJ and McNamara to be attacked by the IDF. They were sitting ducks, and once Israel began its massacre, the Egyptians would be framed for it (just as Muslim extremists were blamed for 9-11).

Since Nasser was backed by the Soviets, they would ultimately be held responsible for the onslaught, thus giving LBJ a pretext for war. In order to stop Russian expansionism and influence in the region, LBJ and the 303 Committee gave the OK to dispatch fighter planes armed with nuclear weapons aimed at Cairo. They also had at their disposal Contact X, additionally armed with nukes.

Miraculously, the Israeli military was unable to sink the *Liberty*, thus forcing the U.S. to recall its nuclear-laden fighters. If they had bombed Cairo, Russia would have retaliated by possibly targeting Tel Aviv. It's still difficult at this point to know who knew what, who called what shots, and where this entire insane scenario would have led.

However, one particular is certain: Israel still retains possession of the Operation Cyanide files, and uses them as blackmail against the

U.S. whenever they deem it necessary. If anyone ever wonders why Israel holds such a demonic influence over the U.S., these records are one explanation. After all, if the Arab world ever discovered the true role played by the U.S. in assisting Israel during the Six Day War, as well as America's potential plans to nuke Cairo, it would forever harm what is at best a tenuous relation with the oil-rich Arab world.

—Written by VICTOR THORN, June, 2009

USS LIberty sits in Portsmouth, Va., a year before the attack.

Too little, too late: A U.S. Navy ship (background) and helicopter (above bow) prepare to help remove the dead and wounded.

A view of a small portion of the Israeli torpedo hole as seen from the waterline.

The *USS Liberty* limps into Malta for repairs and the recovery of dead sailors still entombed below decks.

Hundreds of rockets and machine gun rounds tore into *Liberty*'s superstructure.

Amazingly, the crew of the *Liberty* kept her afloat despite this massive torpedo hole, 34 dead men and more than 170 injured. Had the story of the attack on the *Liberty* been told—and not suppressed—the heroic actions of the crew and captain to save the ship and the remaining crew would have gone down in the annals of U.S. maritime history.

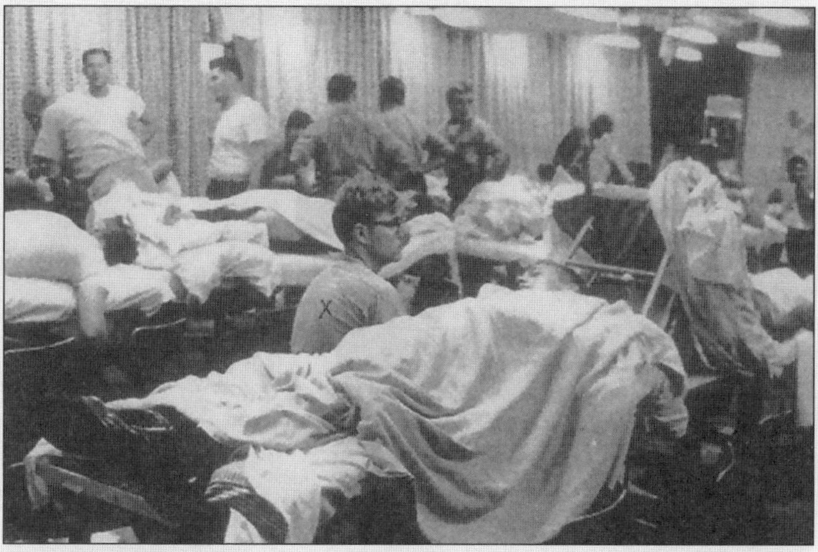

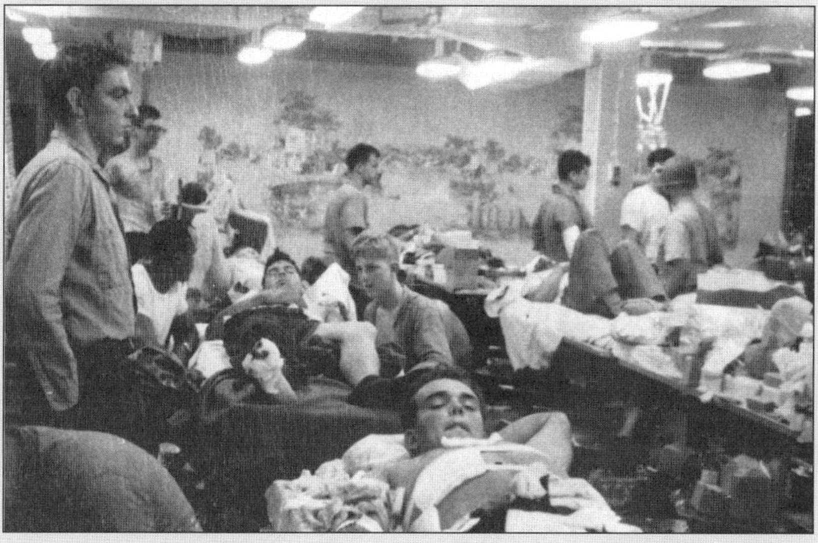

Above are two photos of some of the wounded members of the crew of the *USS Liberty* and their visitors in the mess hall, which had been converted into a makeshift medical ward. More than 171 U.S. servicemen were seriously wounded in the attack. To add insult to serious injury, the men of the *USS Liberty* were ordered to hide details of the attack from the public.

The main blast area from inside the *USS Liberty*.

Above, caskets are brought aboard the *Liberty* that would then carry the bodies of the dead recovered from the area of the ship devastated by the Israeli torpedo and inaccessible to crewmen until *Liberty* got to dry dock in Malta.

Above, Master Chief Stan White, survivor of the attack on the *Liberty*, at a ceremony at Arlington National Cemetery, outside Washington, D.C.

A color guard stands in dress uniform at the mass grave at Arlington National Cemetery bearing the names of six men killed aboard the *Liberty* on June 8, 1967.

High-Ranking Eyewitnesses to the *Liberty* Cover-Up

Overviews/Interviews by Mark Glenn

PHILIP GIRALDI: LBJ's Bizarre Damage Control

Even those who still remember the *USS Liberty* sometimes ask why, 40-some years later, it is important to continue to remind the world what happened on that June day in the eastern Mediterranean. For many, it seems like ancient history in a world that has moved on, a nearly forgotten incident in a nearly forgotten war.

To those people, I usually respond that we Americans both in time of peace and in time of war have always prided ourselves on our moral values. When we call on our soldiers, sailors, and Marines to give their lives for their country, we have an obligation to honor that sacrifice. When one of our ships is wantonly attacked and men die, we have a sacred duty to seek the truth and, once we know the truth, to take the next step, to establish accountability. Without learning the truth and seeking accountability, the deaths of the men who perished on the *Liberty* will have been in vain.

To be sure, the needless deaths of 34 United States sailors and Marines and the wounding of 171 more would be a tragedy at any time and in any place, but there is a particular pain that comes from the knowledge that many of the men could have been saved in their extremity but for the action of the president of the United States. Without even knowing what exactly had happened, President Lyndon B. Johnson immediately engaged in a bizarre damage control that demonstrated that he was more concerned about possibly upsetting a foreign country than he was in protecting his own fellow citizens. And it did not stop there. When the surviving sailors and Marines returned to port, they were served with a gag order forbidding their even discussing what had taken place on that fateful day.

Their brave captain, whose action had prevented the sinking of the ship and massacre of the entire crew, was presented a Medal of Honor, but in secret at a Navy base, not at the White House as was then and is now customary. A naval board of inquiry was convened hastily, required in any attack on a U.S. warship, but the board, headed by Admiral John McCain, father of the senator, was directed to conclude that the incident had been a case of mistaken identity. Since that time, repeated attempts to reopen the hearings on the attack on the *Liberty* have been rebuffed by both presidents and Congress.

The assault on the *Liberty* is, in fact, the only attack on a U.S. Navy ship that has not been the subject of a congressional inquiry. The media has treated the entire affair as an unpleasant conspiracy theory, refusing to take it seriously. The cover-up continues.

There should be no confusion about what happened on that day, particularly given the recent release of National Security Agency intercepts of the voices of the Israeli pilots who carried out the attack. The government of Israel ordered a daylight attack on a U.S. warship that was operating legally and openly in international waters with a large American flag prominently displayed. There were repeated attacks by airplanes and torpedo boats, and the intention was undoubtedly to sink the vessel and kill everyone on board.

Only the extraordinary heroism of the captain and his crew enabled the vessel to survive and limp into port. Many lives would have been saved if the U.S. Navy jets that had been launched to aid the *Liberty* had been allowed to complete their mission.

But Secretary of Defense Robert McNamara—acting under orders from President Johnson—called them back. Some might call the actions of McNamara and Johnson treason, including even the United States Constitution, which carefully defines treasonous behavior and calls for the death penalty; but the two men were never held accountable.

The cover-up has gone on since that time. Ignoring a wealth of evidence and first person testimony, Israel has called the attack an accident, paid a small sum in reparations, and has never been held accountable for what was a deliberate act of war against the U.S.

Israel's friends in the media, in Congress, and in the White House have made sure that there will never be an official inquiry. Congress would rather appease Israel than remember the sailors and Marines who died in service to their country. But sometimes the truth will come out in spite of efforts to suppress it.

Brave men drawn from among the *Liberty*'s survivors have begun to speak out. They do not consider the cover-up to be good enough, and they want to see their former shipmates remembered and properly honored for their heroism. They also want to see some accountability, for Israel to open its defense archives to reveal what it did and why it did it.

If any of the Israeli leaders who ordered the attack are still alive, they must be tried for the war crime that they surely committed, and they must answer for their decision to attack the United States.

This book, *Ship Without a Country*, is a vital part of the *Liberty* story. Americans should read it and remember the suffering and sacrifice, described in detail by *Liberty* survivors. And after they read it, they should think about what comes next—first the truth, and then the accountability. It is time for Congress and the White House to remember the *USS Liberty*. It is time for the American government to demand some answers from Israel. The families, friends, and shipmates of 34 dead Americans want to know why they died.

—Interview originally conducted by Mark Glenn, July 2009

* * *

Philip M. Giraldi is a former CIA counter-terrorism specialist and military intelligence officer who served 19 years overseas in Turkey, Italy, Germany, and Spain. He was chief of base in Barcelona from 1989 to 1992 and served as official liaison to the Spanish security and intelligence services. Since 1992, Phil has been engaged in security consulting for a number of Fortune 500 corporate clients. He has been designated by the General Accountability Office as an expert on the impact of illegal immigration on terrorism. As a counter-terrorism expert, he has been interviewed by the Canadian Broadcasting Corporation, the British Broadcasting Corporation, Britain's Independent Television Network, FOX News, Polish National Television, Croatian National Television, al-Jazeerah, al-Arabiya, and 60 Minutes. *Mr. Giraldi was awarded an MA and PhD from the University of London in European History and holds a bachelor of arts with honors from the University of Chicago. He speaks Spanish, Italian, German, and Turkish.*

CAPTAIN WARD BOSTON: Set the Record Straight

"Son, I spent two years as a special agent in the FBI and over 30 years in the military, and if there is one thing I learned through all of this, it's that when you get an order, you say 'yes sir' and carry it out with no questions asked."

This was the response given by Captain Ward Boston, USN (Ret) in a series of interviews he gave for *American Free Press* newspaper shortly before he died. For those not familiar with Captain Boston, he played what will one day be recognized as one of the most pivotal roles in recent human history. On June 8th, 1967 he was the senior legal council for the naval board of inquiry concerning the attack on the *USS Liberty* by Israeli air and naval forces resulting in 34 Americans killed and 171 wounded. His job in 1967 was to be part of a hastily called investigation into the attack, and—as he has recently revealed to the shock of many—to rule that Israel's 90-minute blood-fest waged against America's young men was all an "accident" that occurred during "the fog of war," all evidence to the contrary be damned.

In 2002, Captain Boston broke his silence of three decades and released an affidavit to the public in which he admitted that the entire investigation was a sham, and that he was under orders (from persons of no less authority than President Lyndon Johnson and Secretary of Defense Robert McNamara) to rule that the bloodiest day in American naval history since WWII took place as a result of "mistaken identity" and that America's ally, Israel, was innocent of any wrongdoing.

For 35 years Captain Boston lived with the bitter knowledge that his fellow servicemen had been deliberately murdered in what was an act of war by a foreign power, and yet because of the orders he received, was powerless to say anything. A confluence of events, however, led him to make a decision to "damn the torpedoes" and let the chips fall where they may. "I'm an old man," he told AMERICAN FREE PRESS. "They can't threaten my job, and if they throw me into jail, so what? The truth has to be told for the benefit of the survivors and for the American people whose sons and daughters are dying today."

The first of these events leading him to break his silence was the 2002 release of a book entitled *The Liberty Incident,* written by Judge Ahron Jay Cristol, at a time when America was being drawn into a series of long-term military engagements with countries that just so happened to be enemies of Israel. Through his book and subsequent speaking tour, Cristol (a slavish, shameless, fanatical apologist for the Jewish state who is on more-than-friendly terms with a number of people in both the military and arms industry in Israel) did the usual song and dance when it comes to discussing the terrorist state that attacked America in 1967, which was to argue for unconditional acquittal, using a collage of sloppy-yet-deliberate misrepresentations and omissions of fact. In Captain Boston's words, it was Cristol's "insidious attempt to whitewash the event" that pushed him to finally speak out.

"These rats," he said, referring to Israel and her defenders, "they lie about everything. You can't believe a word they say. . . ." What was so important about this statement was that Captain Boston was not just talking about the past, but about the present and future as well. "They've completely infested the entire intelligence and defense apparatus of the United State," he said. "Perle, Feith, Wolfowitz, and all the rest of them. They're spies for Israel, every damned one of them," he said.

"Just consider the five guys who were arrested after 9/11, cheering and celebrating, and then afterwards we come to find out that they were Mossad, and then they get sent back to Israel. They knew all about it, and yet our government, the government I worked for most of my life, did nothing about it. Can you imagine if these guys were Arabs?" he asked. "It's been the same thing ever since 1967," he said with unmistakable agitation. "Protect Israel, protect Israel. . . . In the meantime, our boys are dying over there, and those who don't die are coming back here with all sorts of problems, both physical and psychological."

It was his visit to Israel some years back that clinched it for this man in terms of his feelings for the "great experiment" in Jewish self-rule in the Middle East. "The way they treat the Arabs…it's unconscionable," he said. "You go into Israel, into the only places where they allow the tourists, and it's the picture of paradise, just as the Soviets used to do. Then you take a detour off the approved itinerary and you see what it is really like. The poverty, misery, abuse. Arab kids being gunned down in broad daylight. It's worse than South Africa. Only a person with a ice water in his veins could see the way the Arabs are treated and not be outraged."

As far as the future goes, Captain Boston is not hopeful. "If either they (the Israelis) or the U.S. launches a war against Iran, it will be the beginning of the end," he said. "Armageddon. You'll have Muslims pouring into the area from all over the world, and no army will be able to stop them. They will tear Israel and the Americans to pieces."

Regarding his reaction to the predictable accusations of 'anti-Semitism' that have been leveled against him for telling the truth concerning the attack on the *Liberty*, he laughs it off. "One of my closest friends growing up was Jewish," he said. "I don't have a prejudiced bone in my body. What we are dealing with here is an act of war initiated against the United States, the country I swore an oath to defend, period. If a proper investigation into the attack on the *Liberty* had been allowed to take place and the American people made aware of what happened, we would not be in the middle of this mess in the Middle East now."

—Written by Mark Glenn for AMERICAN FREE PRESS, May 2006

CAPTAIN RICHARD BLOCK: Eyewitness to an Act of War

The outrage in his voice was made all the more striking by his New England accent and Yankee assertiveness that long ago brought about the American Revolution. "I couldn't believe it. One minute, nothing, and then the next minute they were attacking our ship in broad daylight. We had no warning that it was coming, and then 'boom,' there it was, and our guys were being slaughtered."

Like hundreds of other individuals who have particular stories to tell concerning their actions and whereabouts on June 8, 1967, when the *USS Liberty* was attacked by the air and naval forces of Israel, Captain Richard Block's testimony is noteworthy, but in some respects much more important than others. At that time, he was in command of the 6931st Security Group of the USAF Security Services stationed on the island of Crete, where his job was to act as the eyes and ears of the U.S. intelligence community. What he and others under his command heard that day obliterates the lie which has been foisted upon the people of the United States for the last forty years—that the attack was all the result of "mistaken identity"—and proves beyond any reasonable doubt that it was a deliberate and premeditated act of war.

"We were getting the translations in real-time," he said, speaking of the air-to-air and air-to-ground communications taking place between the pilots and C&C (command and control) on the ground in Israel. "They knew it was an American ship. We heard it with our own ears, several times. The story they have told for the last forty years about the *Liberty* being mistaken for another ship is complete bullshit."

Like others who were material witnesses to the act of war that took place that day, Captain Block was told in crystal clear terms to keep his mouth shut concerning what he saw and heard. Shortly thereafter, individuals unknown to him showed up at his post, gathered any documentation dealing with the Israeli intercepts, and hauled them away to be destroyed. And lest anyone fall victim to the typical business that Israel's defenders employ when attempting to cover up her crimes—namely that one man's testimony is "insufficient" evidence in refuting what has been the standard explanation for the last forty years —keep in mind that he is not alone.

Two other individuals contacted by *American Free Press* for this story have related circumstances identical to those of Captain Block, although (for obvious reasons) they insist upon remaining anonymous. According to their statements, they too heard the radio chatter between

Israeli pilots and those on the ground who were giving the orders to attack, and there was no doubt Israel knew unequivocally that it was an American ship and that it was her aim to sink the *Liberty* and leave no survivors, as dead men tell no tales. One individual interviewed for this piece told *American Free Press* that "bets were made" amongst the men in his listening post as to which city in Israel was going to get "nuked first" once the president was made aware of what took place.

As far as Captain Block goes (who has remained silent these last four decades), the event prompting him to speak out was (as in the case of Captain Ward Boston, chief legal council for the Navy's Board of Inquiry) the publication of Jay Ahron Cristol's book, *The Liberty Incident*, which exculpated Israel of any wrongdoing. When Captain Block was made aware of the contents in Cristol's book and heard that the author was going to be at a book signing in a nearby town, he paid him a personal visit to speak his mind. In front of approximately 120 people there that day to hear Cristol run his mouth (including the upper-crust of the town's intelligentsia and politicians), Captain Block got up and said that the book was a pack of lies. "I was there the day that the *Liberty* was attacked, and you weren't," he told a shocked Cristol, whose drooling support for the Jewish state is well known. "I got the raw milk of the intelligence, and all you got was the processed cheese."

Much to his surprise, nothing ill came of Captain Block's confrontation with Cristol. Captain Block has his theories as to why, namely that right now what the "powers that be" want (during a time when American support for Israel is crucial for her existence) is that no attention be drawn to the events of June 8, 1967. "In my opinion," he told *AFP*, "what they want is for all of us to just die off so that the whole *Liberty* thing will become forgotten history."

For Captain Block, though, silence is no longer an acceptable option. "What I want is justice for those guys. What was done to them was an outrage. Personally, I think it was divine providence the ship didn't sink. I am not interested in any notoriety, just justice...justice for our men and for our flag. The bottom line is that this was an act of war perpetrated against the United States, and the American people need to know about it."

Many theories have been offered over the years concerning Israel's motives for attacking the *USS Liberty* that day. Some say it was to cover-up her war crimes in the Sinai desert when she murdered over 250 Egyptian soldiers who had surrendered peaceably. Some say that it was because she was planning to take the Golan Heights in Syria and did not want the news of this impending attack to get out. When asked about what he thought Israel's motives were, Captain Block's answer was simple—That Israel wanted to drag the United States into the war against the Arab countries so that the blood of America's Christians would be spilled rather than that that of Israel's Jews.

In interviewing other survivors of the *USS Liberty*, AFP has learned that some fifteen years after the attack, an Israeli pilot approached some of the servicemen (as well as former Congressman Paul N. (Pete) McCloskey) and revealed to them that as the lead pilot in the attack that day, he recognized the *Liberty* as American and informed his headquarters. Nevertheless, he was told to ignore the American flag and continue his attack. As a result of his refusal to do so, he was immediately arrested after returning to base. Backing up his damning statements are those of former U.S. ambassador to Lebanon, Dwight Porter, who has also stated publicly that the Israeli pilot's radio transmissions were heard by monitors in the U.S. Embassy in Lebanon.

The attack on the *USS Liberty* by air and naval forces of Israel that resulted in the deaths of 34 of America's young men was as much an act of war against the United States as was the "sneak attack" on Pearl Harbor by the Japanese in 1941. The only difference between the two was that the Japanese did not have the machinery in place at that time to cover it up and lie about it as Israel has for the last forty years. Rather than justice, what the American people have been given since that time is lies and further involvement in the tangled affairs of a gangster nation founded on duplicity, genocide, and a mad thirst for world domination. As a reward for the murder of 34 sailors aboard the *Liberty*, Israel—rather than being given a declaration of war by the U.S. Congress—has instead been given (by some accounts) over a trillion dollars with which to further endanger the liberty and security of the American people.

"Better late than never," as the old saying goes, and with that in mind, being that the Congress of the United States refuses to execute its duty with respect to protecting and defending the people and interests of the United States, it is high time that the American people themselves declare that a state of war exists between them and the Jewish state and take all steps necessary in prosecuting this war to a just conclusion. Anything short of this is national suicide, as events taking place today prove on a regular basis.

—Originally written by Mark Glenn
for AMERICAN FREE PRESS on June 6, 2007

Survivor Stories

Overviews/Interviews by Mark Glenn

PHIL TOURNEY: "Staring Into Lucifer's Eyes"

Although raised a Catholic, he never took the idea of the devil's existence seriously until June 8, 1967 when his ship, the *USS Liberty*, was attacked by air and naval forces of the state of Israel in an act of war lasting about the same length of time as the Japanese attack on Pearl Harbor.

"After a two-hour sneak attack involving close to 1,000 rockets, more than 5,000 armor-piercing machine gun bullets, napalm, five torpedoes, and just about every other damned thing you can imagine, the sight of an Israeli helicopter loaded with armed commandos preparing to board the ship brought an even sicker feeling to my gut than what I felt when we were under attack. As the helicopter hovered over the deck at about twenty feet, time stood still. I knew what they were here for: to kill off the crew and then scuttle the ship.

As the helo hovered, I locked eyes with one of the commandos from about fifty feet away. I'll never forget his eyes. They were like the eyes of the devil for all the pity in them. In the moment we locked eyes I knew what he and his buddies were here for, and realized this might be the last chance I had to strike back at the monsters that attacked America. I produced the only weapon I had in my hands at the time, which was my middle finger, and showing no pity for what his comrades in arms had just done to us, he chuckled and gave me the led and gave me the finger back. . . .

And now, 42 years later and much wiser to the ways of the world and to the politics between the U.S. and Israel, I can see that this is how it's been since that day, Israel attacking America, with a smirky smile and a big middle finger stuck right in our face. Zionist control over America is an alien invasion by people who wish us ill, and after what I saw that day, no one will ever be able to convince me of anything different."

He continues—"People ridicule the idea of hell, but I know better. It is real. I've looked into the eyes of the devil in a way up close and personal, beginning June 8, 1967, and every day afterwards. Despite the fact my eardrums were blown out and I am mostly deaf, I still jump a mile high and scream out loud when I hear a car backfire. The smell of burning oil brings me back to the day the ship was on fire.

For people who ask me what it was like, I tell them this—"Imagine being in a small building with no windows and no doors you can't escape from and someone on the outside shooting into it, as the bullets whiz by you just inches away, for two hours. That is a small comparison to what it was like being onboard the *Liberty* as it was attacked that day. Nowhere to run, nowhere to hide as death whizzed by you for two hours, just inches away."

Tourney was in damage control, and on the morning of June 8th was on sounding and security detail, a fancy way of saying roving patrol from 4-8 am. His job was to check everything on the ship and make sure it was functioning properly in the event of any emergency. That morning as he made his rounds, he looked out towards the coastline and knew a war was going on. "Shit was hitting the fan. I was glad it was there and not here. . . . As we heard the explosions on the shore between Israel and the Arabs, my buddy David Skolak and I stood by one of the four .50 caliber machine guns, the only defenses we had, which were basically nothing, and talked about how we would hate to be near one of them if the ship were ever attacked."

Little did he know what was to befall him within less than a minute, because Israel had just finished six hours worth of slow, low-altitude surveillance overflights and had collected all the data on the *Liberty* she needed before the attack. He left Skolak standing near the gun that—along with the antennae—was the first thing taken out when the attack started by unmarked fighter jets. After the first pass, Tourney ran back to where he had left his friend, but saw only a large pool of blood in the gun tube and body parts he assumed were those of Skolak.

Skolak was not the only good friend he would lose in such short time. Ordered by his superiors to put out one of the fires caused by burning napalm, he left his friend Francis Brown for only a minute to find another CO2 canister and, returning to the spot he left his fellow serviceman, slipped and fell to his back on something slimy and wet under his feet. Lying next to his hard landing was a pool of blood his friend lost when he was hit in the back of the head by an Israeli machine gun bullet. Tourney got up, picked up his CO2 canister, emptied it on the burning napalm (to no avail) and threw the empty canister overboard.

Shortly thereafter, he heard the voice of Captain William L. McGonagle ordering the crew to prepare for a torpedo hit on the starboard side. At the time Tourney was one deck above the water line. When the torpedo struck, it picked the ship completely out of the water, followed by a thunderous landing back on the water and an enormous, ear-splitting thud. The ship started to shake and creak, and (as he describes it) sounded like a group of people crying, the metal bending and giving way. Then the ship started listing.

He was ordered below deck to find out where the torpedo hit. The space happened to be where the Communications Technicians worked, an area restricted to almost everyone, including Captain

McGonagle himself. The regular *Liberty* crew—if needed for some maintenance function in the CT spaces—could only enter with an armed Marine escort with orders to shoot them if they were someplace not authorized. When Tourney arrived at the door to the CT space, he found it locked with an electronic keypad. He beat on the door with an ax, telling those inside to open it. The other side said they wouldn't let him enter since he had no authorization. Tourney's response was that if they didn't open the door, he'd beat it down with the axe.

When the door opened, Tourney came to one of the hatches leading to the most secretive place in the CT area and slowly opened it, not knowing if water would rush out and flood his compartment. He could hear the sound of air escaping, indicating that indeed water was filling the area below. Then, when he heard pounding on the other side of the thick metal door, he threw it open, reached down and grabbed a blackened-faced Sergeant Bryce Lockwood USMC, Russian language specialist, and hauled him out.

He then returned topside and saw the torpedo boats from no more than fifty feet away, firing like a bunch of drunken fraternity punks. They shot at anything that moved, including firefighters and stretcher-bearers, just one of the many war crimes perpetrated by Israel that day. While watching all this, Tourney then received news that Captain McGonagle had given the order to prepare to abandon ship.

"The only three life rafts still intact we threw into the water, which were then shot to pieces by the Israelis. Two of them sunk, and I watched as the sons of bitches pulled one onboard their boat as a souvenir. It was then that I knew who they were, because there it was, as big as life, the Star of David flag. The maggots continued circling our ship, shooting until they ran out of bullets. We thought the attack was over."

Once he was confident the attack had ended, Tourney got to work helping the wounded. "There's no other way to describe it other than to say it looked like a slaughterhouse. . . . Oceans of blood, body parts, tops of skulls, gaping holes. Tom Riley had over 500 pieces of shrapnel in him and was covered with haze grey paint, thick as snot, which was a good thing because it kept the blood in his body. The larger body parts were put in body bags.

I was ordered to the officer's mess to assist Doc Kiepfer, who had been badly wounded, although we didn't know it at the time. He was wearing a life vest tied tight around his waist to keep his guts in. Gary Blanchard was on a stretcher, and when he saw me, motioned for me to come over. He asked me to take off his socks because he said his feet were hot. I removed his black socks and this seemed to calm him a little. I held his hand and asked if he wanted water or anything. The only thing he asked was whether or not he was going to live. I shook my head no. I regret that to this day. As I held a battle lantern, a minute later Doc was cutting him open from his chest to his belly button. As soon as he was opened up he was gone. Doc put three stitches in him to hold his guts together, and then he was put into a body bag and we moved on.

Late in the evening as it was getting dark, no one would sleep in their bunks, but insisted on sleeping on the main deck because they were afraid the Israelis would come back, or the ship would break apart with them below. No one slept, though. Instead, we stayed awake all night, plugging holes with wooden pegs since water was coming in everywhere.

When daylight arrived, I got my next grisly task, as Captain ordered me to hose off all the blood and body parts, which included pieces of bone, meat, blood, and a shoe with a foot still in it. It looked like pieces of stew meat, but I knew it wasn't a cow, but rather my shipmates. The blood baked into the paint, and we couldn't clean it all off. I felt guilty for washing my shipmates' body parts over the side, but had to do as told.

As I was washing off the deck, I saw the *USS America* coming towards us over the horizon, along with the *Davis* and *Massey*. Davis pulled up along the starboard side and tied up. I remember the water was very calm. As *Davis* crewmen boarded the *Liberty*, many of them were bawling their eyes out like little kids, begging us to forgive them for not coming to our aid. Then they started unloading the wounded."

Although he didn't realize it at the time, the worst part of the whole ordeal was yet to occur. On the way to Malta for repairs, Admiral Isaac Kidd boarded the *Liberty* and started his "investigation." Interviewing the *Liberty* crew, he was told about the over-flights, the unmarked attacking aircraft, the life rafts being shot up, shooting at stretcher-bearers, et al. Afterwards, he warned the crew of the *Liberty* they would face prison or death if they revealed what had happened the previous day. Tourney summed it up thus—"At that point we all realized we had been set up and were a ship without a country. I was so afraid of what they would do to me if I talked that for years I actually forgot the date it happened."

Once they arrived in Malta and began repairs, all evidence of the attack was erased. Holes made by the rockets, machine guns and—last but certainly not least—the 30x40 torpedo hole, were patched flawlessly. Everything received a fresh coat of paint. The CT space where the torpedo had hit was not painted the usual grey, but rather red to hide the innocent blood that had been spilled. Norfolk was the *Liberty*'s regular port, but she and her crew were sent instead to Little Creek, far away from the media. When the *Liberty* crew arrived they found a few "welcome home" signs, but nothing more. No bands, nothing.

"Immediately after the attack, this became something between me and those who tried to kill me. Now I know it's much bigger. It is my family, my country, and every human being on the planet. The people who tried to murder us that day are not normal or sane. Human life does not mean the same thing to them that it means to the rest of us, something I learned the day we were attacked. We might as well have been ants for all they cared. The Americans are good people, but naïve. We don't know what tyranny is. We are basically an honest, hard-working people without guile, so we have a tough time understanding people who are the opposite; but that is what we're talking about when we speak of Israel and her prostitutes in D.C."

Phil Tourney's last words on the matter are thus—"This is not a conspiracy theory. It is a conspiracy fact. It is written in stone. The truth about the *Liberty* is like a dam bursting at the seams. Once it starts to go, there is no stopping it—like waters that are cleansing, and yet destructive in their power. As much as I know that Jesus Christ was there with us that day and kept us afloat, I also know the attack on the *Liberty* is the key that will open the door to our liberation and the key that will lock the gate on this devil forever, and it won't be a minute too soon.

"If there is one thing I want known by everyone—Americans or otherwise—it is that without the boilermakers—meaning the ship's engineers, Gary Brummett, Gene Owens, JP Newell, and others, we would have gone to the bottom, no doubt. They are the real heroes that day, and yet little attention is paid to what they did. They not only saved the ship, they saved the world, for if Israel had succeeded with what she wanted, it would have been WW III."

* * *

Phillip F. Tourney was an E4 3rd class petty officer on the day the USS Liberty *was attacked. Following his tour on the* USS Liberty, *he served aboard the* USS Maddox, *the ship at the center of the Gulf of Tonkin incident, leading to the infamous escalation of hostilities between the U.S. and Vietnam. As a result of his being aboard the* Liberty *the day it was attacked, he received the Bronze Star with Combat V for Valor, the Purple Heart, the Combat Action Ribbon, the Presidential Unit Citation, the Battle E Efficiency Ribbon, and the National Defense Medal. On none of his decorations was the name "Israel" mentioned, and as a result people thought his citations were phony because the attacking country was not named. He is one of only a few* Liberty *crewmembers to have stayed with the ship from the day it left Norfolk until it returned to the U.S.*

—Interview originally conducted by Mark Glenn, June, 2009

RON KUKAL: "Dead Men Walking"

At the outset of our discussion, he asks the question out loud—"Why did I, along with Phil Tourney and Gary Brummett, make that hard turn and—no matter what the consequences—decide to tell the truth, the whole truth, and nothing but the truth so help us God concerning the *USS Liberty* and everything that happened afterwards, knowing we would come up against a brick wall at every corner? Well, I can't exactly speak for Phil and Gary, although I have my suspicions they would agree, but for me it was simple—love of family, love of my community, love for this nation and what it stands for, and most importantly, for God Himself.

I fought with myself for years over the priorities in one's life. God came first, then wife and kids, then extended family, but where does one's country fit? After the attack on the *Liberty* and the fact that we survivors were left out there, floating in this netherworld between perdition and hell, trying to make sense as to why our own government left us out there to die, both on June 8 and every day afterwards, I had a hard time figuring out where country fit into that list of priorities. Like our vets coming back from 'Nam who were spit on the minute their feet hit American soil, I felt the same way they did—the idea of "country" was an alien idea now. I have no country.

Now, however, 42 years and an ocean of tears later, my mind is clearer and I can differentiate between the idea of "country" as something that abandoned me 42 years ago and the idea of "country" as it is supposed to be. Maybe it's my old age or the fact that I realize that this is what my kids and grandkids are going to inherit, but now I realize that country fits right underneath God Himself, because if there is no country, there is nothing else—no wives, no children, no family, no future. Nothing."

Given the fact that Ron Kukal was in charge of body recovery/identification and that it was his friends down in the CT space accounting for the bulk of the deaths, he can only go so far in describing the events of that day. When he does these interviews, he has to hook up a machine to monitor his blood pressure because of how upsetting it is. He doesn't want the fact that he's discussing these things to kill him, literally. It was in his super-secret compartment where the torpedo struck, killing 25 of his friends instantly. Ron was tasked with the grisly work of piecing together an arm here, a leg there, a head, anything left over and trying to put people back together so they could be given a proper burial.

"When I heard the Captain say over the loudspeaker, 'Prepare for torpedo attack, starboard side,' I knew deep down it was bad news. Time stood still. At once I could feel a heavy hand on my shoulder, pushing me down and a voice screaming at me to hit the floor. Then came the explosion. Our world was instantly opened up to all the immensity of the ocean. Next thing I knew, I was swimming. There was one battle lantern that was lit. The funny thing was that it never [had] worked. The batteries were always going bad or something else. But this time it worked: the light of God. Just like the antennae that never worked, but which saved us that day in getting out a distress signal. Had it not been for that lantern I would have been a goner, because it was right beside the hatch that saved my life. After I got out I ran into Lieutenant Golden, and he ordered me to go back and make sure everyone who could get out did. Had I not been trained to follow orders, I would have told him where to go and done what I wanted.

It's in our human nature to reject pain and to run away from it. We look at those who push us to our limits as enemies, when in actuality they are our best friends. Looking back on what I went through that day and every day since, I applaud the people who trained me in the 1950s, and especially in boot camp.

Chief Shrewsberry. I started out hating this man, but what he taught me kept me alive years later when the *Liberty* was being attacked, although I didn't realize it at the time. The one thing I would say to the NCOs training our young men is this—Please don't change anything in the training. If it ain't broke, don't fix it. We never had the options open to our young servicemen and women today—no stress cards or anything like that. Of course God is on top of all this, no doubt in my mind, but what they taught us back then was how to handle yourself when there wasn't anyone else to handle it for you. Nine weeks of learning how to stay alive in a bad situation. More than that, they taught me how to love this country, which wasn't hard to do, because it's America. . . .

First week of boot camp—we were never allowed to lay in our cot during the daytime. I lay down after lunch one day when an officer came through and ordered me to write myself up. I delivered it to the captain personally, thinking to myself how petty it was. Now I can see it wasn't. The point was: you followed orders to a tee without questions. On Sundays you had two choices—either church, or a write a letter back home. It was a path for the rest of my life.

When I joined, it was a one-way ticket. There was no quitting, negotiating, pleading or otherwise. You WILL do this, was the program, and this was a constitution that lasted for the rest of my life. A lot of the other guys don't realize how much this training has stuck with them all these years, and this is what has kept them sane, if such a thing can be said.

As you get towards the end of your life, you start to take stock of it all. The loss of family, the ingratitude of the country for what we went through, and what we have done since then. I have gone to my knees and told God "I can't do it anymore, but since I can't take my own life, please do it for me." The response has always been the same. "You're not done yet, Ron. You still have work to do," which means I am going to be around until this thing gets done.

The only thing that has slowed me to a crawl—not fear of the enemy or being thrown in jail despite our orders to stay silent. It was when my kids turned their backs on me, and my wife turned them against me for trying to do the right thing. It ground me to a stop. For a person who hasn't experienced the terror of having your own children ripped out of your hands for trying to do the right thing—I can't describe it. It's as indescribable as the miracles that took place the day we were attacked.

At this time in my life, I have gone from hating the people who did this to us to feeling sorry for them. Take McNamara, for example—He is going to take what he knows he did to the grave with him and have to face the ultimate judge one day. Even if he comes clean at the end of his life like Captain Boston [senior counsel to the U.S. Navy court of inquiry investigating the attack] did, he still won't go to God with a peaceful heart. It will torment him forever, and forever is a hell of a long time. How can I not feel sorry for some poor bastard like that? As far as the Israeli pilots and gunners who tried to sink us that day, it will be the same for them. Israel might be able to make deals in this life, but she certainly won't be able to do it in the hereafter. God doesn't negotiate on things like His wrath and His justice.

I don't do this because I am afraid of going to hell. I have seen hell and don't want to be there anymore, and I know my only ticket out of that place is to do what I'm doing now. More than anything else, I want to see my family healed and for the peace we once had to return before I go. . . ."

For Ron, one of the more painful things to deal with these days in trying to tell the story of what took place 42 years ago in Israel's act of war against the United States is the "just let it go" business. "To see the uninterest in their eyes, or worse, when they pretend to be interested. I can't count how many pastors refused to believe me, refused to consider the possibility that dear little Israel could do something like this, and time and again would tell me to forget it. Some even accused me of lying and hallucinating about the whole thing, because it's not possible for God's chosen people to do such things."

Nevertheless, despite the loss of his family and living with the nightmares he still has in trying to piece together the remnants of his fellow communication technicians, Ron maintains his sense of hope. "God will have the final say and the last laugh in all of this. I know it to be true, and it's for this reason I meditate often on the final verse from the *Book of Malachi,* the last book of the Old Testament before the arrival of Jesus that reads of rejuvenation and judgment."

"I will send the prophet Elijah to you before that great and dreadful day of the Lord's judgment, and He will turn the hearts of the parents to their children, and the hearts of the children to their parents; or else I will come and strike the land with total destruction."

—Interview originally conducted by Mark Glenn, June, 2009

* * *

Ron Kukal was an E6 1st class petty officer who worked for the National Security Agency. Being that the USS Liberty *was a spy ship capable of picking up any electronic transmission in the world, his job as a communications technician involved handling the most highly classified information available. He was in the CT space that received the blast of an Israeli torpedo re-*

sulting in the instant deaths of 25 of his fellow CTs. He is the recipient of the Purple Heart, Presidential Unit Citation, the Combat Action Ribbon, and the Navy efficiency medal.

BRYCE LOCKWOOD: "Out to kill every one of us?"

Of the many people I had wanted to meet during my weekend with the *USS Liberty* survivors, near the top of the list was Sergeant Bryce Lockwood. Ever since reading about him in various books and articles written on what took place, the story was that he had saved several guys that day, dragging them out of the lower room where an Israeli missile had penetrated the ship's hull, and then exploded.

And then, in the blink of an eye, my plane landed at Reagan National Airport. There he was, standing before me in the lobby of the hotel where the reunion was taking place. As politely as I could, I extended my hand to Sergeant Lockwood. He grabbed my hand with startling firmness, one might almost say with mild violence, as if I were one of the guys he was pulling to safety that day. He then fixed his large, grayish-blue eyes on mine, and in a mask of barely-concealed rage, said to me, "You know they were out to kill us that day. . . . You know that, don't you? Every damned one of us!"

An air of uncomfortableness—if indeed that is the correct word—came over our small group as we stood there. The other fellows stopped chattering and got quiet, lowered their heads and moved their hands semi-prayerfully toward their midsections in respectful deference to what Bryce was saying.

What I came to understand in an instant was that this was a well-known exercise on their part, something they had dealt with many times before in their 40 years together. They had come to recognize when someone was having an "episode" where a hurricane of emotions were raging within them, and that every other trivial thing taking place at that moment needed to stop so that the guy could purge himself of his demons.

Sergeant Lockwood continued his grip on my hand, maintaining his furious, unblinking stare into my eyes as if to say, "Why, young man? Can you tell me why? Why did they do this to us?"

Out of respect for what he was going through at that moment, I did not blink or flinch. It was obvious to me that this man has been living in hell since that day, a day that I was crawling around on the floor in diapers. I was moved to immediate, unconditional compassion for him. I stood there, not moving, holding on to his hand as long and as tight as he held on to mine. I continued staring at him and allowed him to continue staring at me, and once I sensed he had gotten it out of his system, I simply nodded sympathetically to him and said, "I know, Sergeant, and may God damn them for what they did to you that day. . . ."

No longer in the grip of his anger, he was now like a little child in the grip of the same despair he had dealt with the previous 40 years; that terrible place where he wails out loud the question "WHY?!" over and over.

In reverent silence I watched as he was led away by his lovely wife Louise to a quiet, private corner of the hotel lobby. The chatter slowly began anew where it had left off. I, however, kept my eyes on him, glancing sideways, his shoulders heaving up and down convulsively as he wept like a child. For her part, Louise—no doubt as she had done millions of times previously—simply did what she could and rubbed his back with the best sympathy she could muster as a wife who understands as much about the pain of battle as a husband understands the pain of childbirth.

—Originally written by Mark Glenn, June 2007

U.S. Servicemen With a Story to Tell . . .
Censored by the U.S. Government . . .
Ordered to Keep Their Mouths Shut . . .
But They Won't Stay Silent Any Longer!

SHIP WITHOUT A COUNTRY

When one considers that thousands of books, articles, essays, documentaries, and blockbuster films have been made concerning pivotal events in history such as Pearl Harbor and the assassination of JFK; at the same time we need to ask: why has no such attention towards the attack on the *USS Liberty* (June 8, 1967) taken place? After all, had the ship been sunk as planned, it would have kicked off a monumental (possibly nuclear) exchange between the US and USSR.

The reason for this silence over the *Liberty* attack is simple. It didn't go off as planned, meaning the ship was not sunk. More importantly, the entity responsible for this attack was the most sacred of all sacred cows--Israel. Moreover, any rational person that spent even five minutes considering the facts of this event would walk away concluding that it was a deliberate act of war against the United States.

In this book, readers will come into contact with many of these facts-- disturbing items that have been kept deliberately, some might even say fanatically hidden, for nearly half a century. They paint the ultimate picture of set-up, betrayal, and cover-up; both by Israel and elements within the U.S. government of an event that, had it gone as planned, would have irrevocably changed life as the world knows it. Softcover, 90 pages, #SWC, $15.

Order from American Free Press, 645 Pennsylvania Avenue SE, Suite 100, Washington, D.C. 20003. No charge for S&H inside the U.S. Call AFP toll free at 1-888-699-NEWS to charge to Visa or MasterCard.

TARGET TRAFICANT: The Outrageous Story of How the Justice Department, the Israeli Lobby and the American Mass Media Conspired to Set Up and Take Down Congressman Jim Traficant—by Michael Collins Piper. The Traficant case is the most outrageous hit-and-run operation ever orchestrated against a U.S. public official. Piper dissects the intrigues of the Justice Department and the FBI and shows that the congressman was innocent of all of the charges. **Softcover, 176 pages, $25.**

THE HIGH PRIESTS OF WAR: The Secret History of America's Neo-Cons—The High Priests of War, by Michael Collins Piper, tells the secret history of how America's neo-conservatives came to power and orchestrated the war against Iraq as the first step in their drive for global power. Softcover, 144 pages, $20.

DIRTY SECRETS: Crime, Conspiracy & Cover-Up During the 20th Century—Here's a fascinating collection of writings from Michael Collins Piper, transcripts of uncensored radio interviews and reviews of his works—all compiled in one volume. Read where Piper's investigations have led him on such explosive topics as the Martin Luther King and JFK assassinations, the Oklahoma City bombing, the attack on the *Liberty* and many more. Softcover, 256 pages, $22.

THE JUDAS GOATS: The Shocking Never-Before-Told Story of the Infiltration and Subversion of the American Nationalist Movement—BY MICHAEL COLLINS PIPER—Here is a detailed overview of the intrigues of the infamous Anti-Defamation League of B'nai B'rith, the corruption of the FBI and the CIA by Zionist elements, the evidence pointing toward Israeli involvement in the OKC bombing, the strange, little-known story of how Trotskyites seized command of the American "conservative" movement and also played a role in manipulating Sen. Joseph R. McCarthy's hunt for communists. Softcover, 376 pages, $25 per copy.

THE NEW JERUSALEM: Zionist Power in America—This explosive study contains all of the solid facts and figures documenting the massive accumulation of wealth and power by those who have used that influence to direct the course of American affairs—the forces behind America's "New Imperialism." While there are many historical books on "the Israeli lobby," this is unique. Another classic by Michael Collins Piper. Softcover, 184 pages, $20.

FUTURE FASTFORWARD: The Zionist Anglo-American Empire Meltdown—Is global "Empire Capitalism" about to come crashing down? Will there be a worldwide "people's war" against the Zionists and their powerful minions? Is nuclear war inevitable? What retribution will be meted out to those people who have foisted New World Order slavery upon the people of the world? By Asian political figure Matthias Chang. Softcover, 400 pages, $25.

BRAINWASHED FOR WAR: Programmed to Kill—From the Cold War to Vietnam and now the "War Against Terror" we have been lied to, mind-controlled and duped by a power elite with the goal of making us mindless supporters of bloody war. By Matthias Chang. Softcover, 556 pages, $30.

SHADOW MONEYLENDERS: And the Global Financial Tsunami—Here is an expose of the "Shadow Moneylenders" and how they amassed a $500 trillion empire while much of the world lost its shirt. Written before the 2008-09 financial collapse, author and financial advisor Matthias Chang predicted it all. Softcover, 350 pages, $30.

NO BEAUTY IN THE BEAST: Israel Without Her Mascara—Author Mark Glenn examines Israel from a politically incorrect perspective and comes to the conclusion that the beast of John's Revelation is in fact the beast of Zionist supremacy—a beast that is now devouring the world. Also an amazing chapter of quotes from the perpetrators themselves. Must read for all who call themselves Christians. Softcover, 302 pages, $25.

PHANTOM FLIGHT 93 and Other Astounding September 11 Mysteries Explored. By Victor Thorn and Lisa Guliani. A collection of interviews, articles and on-the-scene investigations by Thorn and Guliani expose the government cover-up of the fate of Flight 93 (the Shanksville flight) as pure fiction. WHat really happened? Softcover, 150 pages, #1575, $20.

THE CIA IN IRAN: The 1953 Coup & the Origins of the US-Iran Divide reveals how U.S. and British operatives employed every dirty trick at their disposal, including bribery, murder and terrorism, to topple the democratically elected government of Prime Minister Mohammad Mossadeq and maneuvered the infamous Shah of Iran into power. Softcover, 150 pages, #1575, $20.

JIM TUCKER'S BILDERBERG DIARY. AFP editor and reporter Jim Tucker has spent the last 25 years tracking down a group of the richest and most influential industrialists, bankers, media moguls and world leaders that meets every year in complete secrecy in some of the poshest venues the world has to offer. Only Tucker has penetrated these meetings and reported on the nefarious goings on inside despite armed guards, attack dogs and barbed wire fences. Softcover, 272 pages, $25.

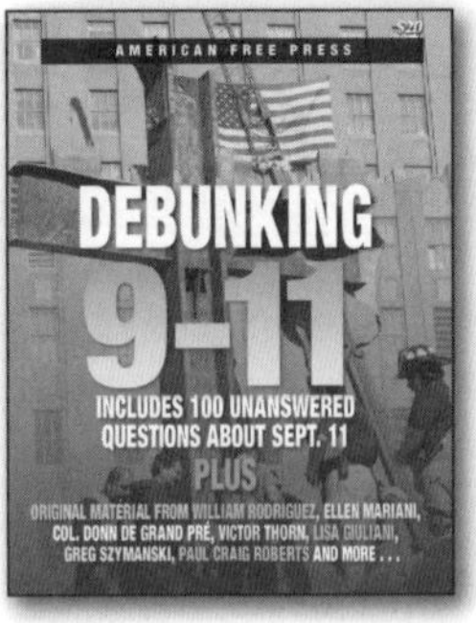

DEBUNKING 9-11: 100 Unanswered Questions About September 11. All of AFP's groundbreaking coverage of the event from the beginning: the spies operating in New York; the many theories put forth by independent researchers who reject the government's explanation of many of the events of Sept. 11; alternative theories as to why the twin towers collapsed; detailed information of foreknowledge by the government and foreign intelligence agencies; and much, much more. Large-sized (8.5″ x 11″ format), 108 pages, $20. Many high-quality photos.

THE PASSION PLAY AT OBERAMMERGAU—How the Thought Police Censored Jesus. Find out how the German citizens of Oberammergau, Germany, were forced by the Zionist thought police to change their Passion Play—performed since the 1600s—to make it "less offensive." A shocker. Includes the full text of the play in novel form. Softcover, 225 pages, $20. Many photos.

THE IMMORALITY OF ILLEGAL IMMIGRATION: An Alternative Christian View. Father Patrick Bascio, a devout Catholic priest, has watched as Christian churches—both Catholic and Protestant—have turned a blind eye toward illegal immigration, ignoring the major moral ramifications of the alien invasion. Gang violence, broken homes, joblessness, national security concerns—Bascio addresses them all in this hard-hitting book. Softcover, 180 pages, #IM, $25.

PERFIDY: THE CABAL THAT BETRAYED OUR POWS. Two high-ranking congressmen—John McCain and John Kerry—who both served in the U.S. military, are named as two of the biggest culprits in the official effort to hide the truth from the public about U.S. POWs purposely left behind and abandoned by our government as part of an official U.S. policy of appeasement. Written by Sgt. John Top Holland and Father Patrick Bascio. Softcover, 225 pages, #PB, $25.

ORDER ANY OR ALL of these books from AMERICAN FREE PRESS, 645 Pennsylvania Avenue SE, Suite 100, Washington, D.C. 20003. To charge to Visa or MasterCard by phone, call 1-888-699-NEWS (6397) toll free. See more books online at AmericanFreePress.net. For bulk pricing on any of these books, please call AFP at 202-544-5977 for lowest available multiple-copy price. No charge for S&H inside the U.S.—in most cases. Outside the U.S. please add $5 per book S&H.

SUBSCRIBE TO *AMERICAN FREE PRESS* NEWSPAPER AND GET FREE BOOKS!

AMERICAN FREE PRESS ORDERING COUPON

Item#	Description/Title	Qty	Cost Ea.	Total
			SUBTOTAL	
			S&H: No S&H inside U.S. Outside U.S. add $6 per book	
			Send a 1-year subscription to AFP for $59 plus 1 free book*	
			Send a 2-year subscription to AFP for $99 plus 2 free books**	
			TOTAL	

***NOTE ABOUT FREE BOOKS: For a one-year subscription to *American Free Press* newspaper ($59), we'll send you one free copy of Michael Collins Piper's *The High Priests of War*. **For a two-year subscription we'll send you *The High Priests of War* PLUS *The New Jerusalem: Zionist Power in America*—almost $40 in free books! (Domestic USA only.)**

PAYMENT OPTIONS: ❏ CHECK/MO ❏ VISA ❏ MASTERCARD

Card # ______________________________

Expiration Date ______________ Signature ______________________

USS99

CUSTOMER INFORMATION:

NAME ______________________________

ADDRESS ______________________________

CIty/STATE/ZIP ______________________________

RETURN WITH PAYMENT TO: AMERICAN FREE PRESS, 645 Pennsylvania Avenue SE, Suite 100, Washington, D.C. 20003. Call 1-888-699-NEWS (6397) toll free to charge a subscription or books to Visa or MasterCard.